Our Faith

Ecumenical Creeds,
Reformed Confessions,
and Other Resources

Our Faith

Ecumenical Creeds,
Reformed Confessions,
and Other Resources

Including
the Doctrinal Standards
of the
Christian Reformed Church in North America
and the
Reformed Church in America

FAITH
ALIVE®
Christian Resources

Grand Rapids, Michigan

We welcome your comments. Call us at 1-800-333-8300 or e-mail us at editors@faithaliveresources.org.

ISBN 978-1-59255-725-7

10 9 8 7 6 5 4 3 2 1

Contents

Preface and Acknowledgments

This book gathers in one volume all the creeds and confessions of the Reformed Church in America (RCA) and the Christian Reformed Church in North America (CRC).

The creeds of both the CRC and RCA (along with many other Christian churches worldwide) are the time-tested and honored Apostles' Creed, Nicene Creed, and Athanasian Creed.

The editions of the three historic Reformation confessions in this book—the Belgic Confession, the Heidelberg Catechism, and the Canons of Dort—are new translations completed jointly by the RCA and the CRC (with help from the Presbyterian Church [USA] on the Heidelberg Catechism). Within these confessions, the RCA and CRC have added explanatory footnotes or amended the text in a few places. We thank the following for their important and faithful work on the joint translation committee:

- Lyle Bierma (CRC, Calvin Theological Seminary)
- J. Todd Billings (RCA, Western Theological Seminary)
- Eugene Heideman (RCA, Western Theological Seminary, emeritus)
- Charles White (RCA staff)
- Leonard J. Vander Zee (CRC staff)
- Dawn Devries (Union Presbyterian Seminary)
- David Stubbs (Western Theological Seminary)

Also included in this book is the more recent Belhar Confession (1986), adopted as a full confession by the RCA in 2010 and as an Ecumenical Faith Declaration by the CRC in 2012.

In addition, we have included two contemporary statements of faith that stand alongside the confessions but do not have confessional status. These are *Our Song of Hope* (RCA, 1978) and *Our World Belongs to God: A Contemporary Testimony* (CRC, 2008).

It is our prayer that this collection will deepen the faith of our churches, further unite us in our common confessions, and serve as a testimony to the historic Reformed faith as a gift to the whole church.

—Leonard J. Vander Zee, Theological Editor,
Faith Alive Christian Resources

Introduction

For Reformed Christians, the Bible alone is the final authority for faith and practice. There is no other book that holds equal status to the Bible, for as the Belgic Confession so elegantly states, although we come to know God through the "beautiful book" of creation, "God makes himself known to us more clearly by his holy and divine Word, as much as we need in this life, for God's glory and for our salvation." The triune God speaks and acts uniquely through Scripture, using this instrument of revelation to conform his people to the image of Christ.

But how should we as Christians interpret the Bible? This is necessarily a theological question, for we cannot (and should not) pretend to approach Scripture without a faith that seeks understanding. Precisely because of the uniqueness and centrality of Scripture we cannot leave creeds and confessions behind. We are called to confess the Christian faith—a faith that is not simply the expression of our individual desires and needs but that believes the triune God is active in the church and the world, and speaks to us through Scripture. The ecumenical creeds and Reformed confessions, most arising from the crucible of theological struggle and at times fierce persecution, continue to guide our faith by returning us again and again to the heart of the revelation of the triune God in his Word.

Indeed, precisely because we value Scripture, we should turn with expectancy to the creeds and confessions of the church. We are all people of our own age. But the Holy Spirit who inspires Scripture and illumines its reading is not just the Spirit of our day. Together we share in the ongoing presence and work of the Spirit who was given to the church to guide it into the truth throughout its long history. Thus, if we are to read Scripture in a way that is open to the Spirit's life-giving and countercultural illumination in our age, we cannot be content with reading Scripture only through the lens of our contemporary situation. We need to read Scripture with those who have come before—and the creeds and confessions give us access to the wisdom of our forebears.

The Reformed tradition, as represented by its confessions, sees itself as catholic—not in the sense of being "Roman Catholic" but in its participation in the "one holy catholic and apostolic church" as confessed in the Nicene Creed. As such, the Reformed tradition does not seek to reinvent the wheel when it comes to core catholic doctrines derived from Scripture, such as the Holy Trinity. Indeed, at the conclusion of two articles on the Trinity, the Belgic Confession notes its common confession with the universal church, saying that "we willingly accept the three ecumenical creeds—the Apostles', Nicene, and Athanasian—as well as what the ancient fathers decided in agreement with them" (Art. 9). Being Reformed does not mean that we cling as individuals to the Bible in a way that ignores the long tradition of Christian teaching that stretches back to the early church. Instead, as Reformed churches we join together with the universal church in confessing the biblical teaching of these creeds.

In addition, the Reformed confessions provide us with vital scriptural interpretation that gives us a broad view of the gospel, revealing the contours of historic Christian teaching from a Reformed perspective. And for people who value Scripture highly, the confessions are a key witness to the teaching of Scripture because we cannot (and should not) approach Scripture as though we were blank slates. Since we always bring presuppositions to the Bible, the confessions serve to shape our understanding in faithful ways and provide a needed theological lens for interpreting Scripture's message. Forged in the deep study and intense struggle of the saints who have gone before us, the creeds and Reformed confessions strengthen our witness to the biblical gospel today.

The jointly translated Reformation confessions in this book represent a celebration of shared heritage and the promise of contemporary ecumenical fellowship. Building on the insights of ongoing historical inquiry and rendered in contemporary English, the shared edition of these confessions anchors us in the deep insights and scriptural interpretations of our past, even as we continue the conversation with others who share in the rich and multifaceted Reformed tradition today.

—J. Todd Billings, Associate Professor of Reformed Theology,
Western Theological Seminary

Ecumenical Creeds

Apostles' Creed

This creed is called the Apostles' Creed not because it was produced by the apostles themselves but because it contains a brief summary of their teachings. It sets forth their doctrine, as the German scholar Philip Schaff put it, "in sublime simplicity, in unsurpassable brevity, in the most beautiful order, and with liturgical solemnity" (History of the Apostolic Church, p. 568.) In its present form the Apostles' Creed is dated no later than the fourth century. More than any other Christian creed, it may justly be called an ecumenical symbol of faith.

I believe in God, the Father almighty,
    creator of heaven and earth.

I believe in Jesus Christ, his only Son, our Lord,*
    who was conceived by the Holy Spirit
    and born of the virgin Mary.
    He suffered under Pontius Pilate,
    was crucified, died, and was buried;
    he descended to hell.
    The third day he rose again from the dead.
    He ascended to heaven
    and is seated at the right hand of God the Father almighty.
    From there he will come to judge the living and the dead.

I believe in the Holy Spirit,
    the holy catholic** church,
    the communion of saints,
    the forgiveness of sins,
    the resurrection of the body,
    and the life everlasting. Amen.

*in the Heidelberg Catechism within this volume, this line reads ". . . his only begotten Son, our Lord"

**that is, the true Christian church of all times and all places

Nicene Creed

The Nicene Creed, also called the Niceno-Constantinopolitan Creed, is a statement of the orthodox faith of the early Christian church in opposition to certain heresies, especially Arianism. These heresies, which disturbed the church during the fourth century, concerned the doctrine of the Trinity and of the person of Christ. Both the Greek (Eastern) and the Latin (Western) church held this creed in honor, though with one important difference: the Western church insisted on the inclusion of the phrase "and the Son" (known as the "filioque") in the article on the procession of the Holy Spirit; this phrase still is repudiated by the Eastern Orthodox Church. In its present form this creed goes back partially to the Council of Nicea (A.D. 325) with additions by the Council of Constantinople (A.D. 381). It was accepted in its present form at the Council of Chalcedon in 451, but the "filioque" phrase was not added until 589. However, the creed is in substance an accurate and majestic formulation of the Nicene faith.

Nicene Creed (RCA Version)

We believe in one God,
   the Father, the Almighty,
   maker of heaven and earth,
   of all that is, seen and unseen.

We believe in one Lord, Jesus Christ,
   the only Son of God,
   eternally begotten of the Father,
   God from God, Light from Light,
   true God from true God,
   begotten, not made,
   of one being with the Father;
   through him all things were made.
For us and for our salvation
     he came down from heaven:
     was incarnate of the Holy Spirit and the Virgin Mary,
   and became truly human.
For our sake he was crucified under Pontius Pilate;
   he suffered death and was buried.
   On the third day he rose again
     in accordance with the Scriptures;
   he ascended into heaven
     and is seated at the right hand of the Father.
   He will come again in glory to judge the living and the dead,
     and his kingdom will have no end.

We believe in the Holy Spirit, the Lord, the giver of life,
    who proceeds from the Father [and the Son]*,
    who with the Father and the Son is worshiped and glorified,
    who has spoken through the prophets.
    We believe in one holy catholic and apostolic Church.
    We acknowledge one baptism for the forgiveness of sins.
    We look for the resurrection of the dead,
        and the life of the world to come. Amen.

*The RCA translation puts "and the Son" in brackets, in recognition that the "filioque" phrase was not included in the early Greek and Latin versions of the creed.

Nicene Creed (CRC Version)

(This translation of the Greek text was approved by the CRC Synod of 1988.)

We believe in one God,
    the Father almighty,
    maker of heaven and earth,
    of all things visible and invisible.

And in one Lord Jesus Christ,
    the only Son of God,
    begotten from the Father before all ages,
        God from God,
        Light from Light,
        true God from true God,
    begotten, not made;
    of the same essence as the Father.
    Through him all things were made.
    For us and for our salvation
        he came down from heaven;
        he became incarnate by the Holy Spirit and the virgin Mary,
        and was made human.
        He was crucified for us under Pontius Pilate;
        he suffered and was buried.
        The third day he rose again, according to the Scriptures.
        He ascended to heaven
        and is seated at the right hand of the Father.
        He will come again with glory
        to judge the living and the dead.
        His kingdom will never end.

And we believe in the Holy Spirit,
    the Lord, the giver of life.
    He proceeds from the Father and the Son,
    and with the Father and the Son is worshiped and glorified.
    He spoke through the prophets.
    We believe in one holy catholic and apostolic church.
    We affirm one baptism for the forgiveness of sins.
    We look forward to the resurrection of the dead,
    and to life in the world to come. Amen.

Athanasian Creed

This creed is named after Athanasius (A.D. 293-373), the champion of orthodoxy against Arian attacks on the doctrine of the Trinity. Although Athanasius did not write this creed and it is improperly named after him, the name persists because until the seventeenth century it was commonly ascribed to him. It is not from Greek (Eastern) but from Latin (Western) origin, and it is not recognized by the Eastern Orthodox Church today. Apart from the opening and closing sentences, this creed consists of two parts, the first setting forth the orthodox doctrine of the Trinity, and the second dealing chiefly with the incarnation and the two-natures doctrine.

Athanasian Creed (CRC Version)
(This translation was adopted by the CRC Synod of 1988.)

Whoever desires to be saved should above all hold to the catholic faith.

Anyone who does not keep it whole and unbroken will doubtless perish eternally.

Now this is the catholic faith:

That we worship one God in trinity and the trinity in unity,
neither blending their persons
nor dividing their essence.
    For the person of the Father is a distinct person,
    the person of the Son is another,
    and that of the Holy Spirit still another.
    But the divinity of the Father, Son, and Holy Spirit is one,
    their glory equal, their majesty coeternal.

What quality the Father has, the Son has, and the Holy Spirit has.
    The Father is uncreated,
    the Son is uncreated,
    the Holy Spirit is uncreated.

    The Father is immeasurable,
    the Son is immeasurable,
    the Holy Spirit is immeasurable.

    The Father is eternal,
    the Son is eternal,
    the Holy Spirit is eternal.

    And yet there are not three eternal beings;
    there is but one eternal being.
    So too there are not three uncreated or immeasurable beings;
    there is but one uncreated and immeasurable being.

Similarly, the Father is almighty,
the Son is almighty,
the Holy Spirit is almighty.
    Yet there are not three almighty beings;
    there is but one almighty being.

Thus the Father is God,
the Son is God,
the Holy Spirit is God.
    Yet there are not three gods;
    there is but one God.

Thus the Father is Lord,
the Son is Lord,
the Holy Spirit is Lord.
    Yet there are not three lords;
    there is but one Lord.

Just as Christian truth compels us
to confess each person individually
as both God and Lord,
so catholic religion forbids us
to say that there are three gods or lords.

The Father was neither made nor created nor begotten from anyone.
The Son was neither made nor created;
he was begotten from the Father alone.
The Holy Spirit was neither made nor created nor begotten;
he proceeds from the Father and the Son.

Accordingly there is one Father, not three fathers;
there is one Son, not three sons;
there is one Holy Spirit, not three holy spirits.

Nothing in this trinity is before or after,
nothing is greater or smaller;
in their entirety the three persons
are coeternal and coequal with each other.

So in everything, as was said earlier,
we must worship their trinity in their unity
and their unity in their trinity.

Anyone then who desires to be saved
should think thus about the trinity.

But it is necessary for eternal salvation
that one also believe in the incarnation
of our Lord Jesus Christ faithfully.

Now this is the true faith:

That we believe and confess
that our Lord Jesus Christ, God's Son,
is both God and human, equally.

He is God from the essence of the Father,
begotten before time;
and he is human from the essence of his mother,
born in time;
completely God, completely human,
with a rational soul and human flesh;
equal to the Father as regards divinity,
less than the Father as regards humanity.

Although he is God and human,
yet Christ is not two, but one.
He is one, however,
not by his divinity being turned into flesh,
but by God's taking humanity to himself.

He is one,
certainly not by the blending of his essence,
but by the unity of his person.
For just as one human is both rational soul and flesh,
so too the one Christ is both God and human.

He suffered for our salvation;
he descended to hell;
he arose from the dead;
he ascended to heaven;
he is seated at the Father's right hand;
from there he will come to judge the living and the dead.
At his coming all people will arise bodily
and give an accounting of their own deeds.
Those who have done good will enter eternal life,
and those who have done evil will enter eternal fire.

This is the catholic faith:
one cannot be saved without believing it firmly and faithfully.

Athanasian Creed (RCA Version)

Whoever wants to be saved should above all cling to the catholic faith.

Whoever does not guard it whole and inviolable will doubtless perish eternally.

Now this is the catholic faith: We worship one God in trinity and the Trinity in unity, neither confusing the persons nor dividing the divine being.

For the Father is one person, the Son is another, and the Spirit is still another.

But the deity of the Father, Son, and Holy Spirit is one, equal in glory, coeternal in majesty.

What the Father is, the Son is, and so is the Holy Spirit.

Uncreated is the Father; uncreated is the Son; uncreated is the Spirit.

The Father is infinite; the Son is infinite; the Holy Spirit is infinite.

Eternal is the Father; eternal is the Son; eternal is the Spirit: And yet there are not three eternal beings, but one who is eternal; as there are not three uncreated and unlimited beings, but one who is uncreated and unlimited.

Almighty is the Father; almighty is the Son; almighty is the Spirit: And yet there are not three almighty beings, but one who is almighty.

Thus the Father is God; the Son is God; the Holy Spirit is God: And yet there are not three gods, but one God.

Thus the Father is Lord; the Son is Lord; the Holy Spirit is Lord: And yet there are not three lords, but one Lord.

As Christian truth compels us to acknowledge each distinct person as God and Lord, so catholic religion forbids us to say that there are three gods or lords.

The Father was neither made nor created nor begotten; the Son was neither made nor created, but was alone begotten of the Father; the Spirit was neither made nor created, but is proceeding from the Father and the Son.

Thus there is one Father, not three fathers; one Son, not three sons; one Holy Spirit, not three spirits.

And in this Trinity, no one is before or after, greater or less than the other; but all three persons are in themselves, coeternal and coequal; and so we must worship the Trinity in unity and the one God in three persons.

Whoever wants to be saved should think thus about the Trinity.

It is necessary for eternal salvation that one also faithfully believe that our Lord Jesus Christ became flesh.

For this is the true faith that we believe and confess: That our Lord Jesus Christ, God's Son, is both God and man.

He is God, begotten before all worlds from the being of the Father, and he is man, born in the world from the being of his mother—existing fully as God, and fully as man with a rational soul and a human body; equal to the Father in divinity, subordinate to the Father in humanity.

Although he is God and man, he is not divided, but is one Christ.

He is united because God has taken humanity into himself; he does not transform deity into humanity.

He is completely one in the unity of his person, without confusing his natures.

For as the rational soul and body are one person, so the one Christ is God and man.

He suffered death for our salvation. He descended into hell and rose again from the dead.

He ascended into heaven and is seated at the right hand of the Father.

He will come again to judge the living and the dead.

At his coming all people shall rise bodily to give an account of their own deeds.

Those who have done good will enter eternal life, those who have done evil will enter eternal fire.

This is the catholic faith.

One cannot be saved without believing this firmly and faithfully.

Confessions

The Belgic Confession

Introduction

The oldest of the doctrinal standards of the Christian Reformed Church and the Reformed Church in America is the Confession of Faith, popularly known as the Belgic Confession, following the seventeenth-century Latin designation "Confessio Belgica." "Belgica" referred to the whole of the Netherlands, both north and south, which today is divided into the Netherlands and Belgium. The confession's chief author was Guido de Brès, a preacher of the Reformed churches of the Netherlands, who died a martyr to the faith in the year 1567. During the sixteenth century the churches in this country were exposed to terrible persecution by the Roman Catholic government. To protest against this cruel oppression, and to prove to the persecutors that the adherents of the Reformed faith were not rebels, as was laid to their charge, but law-abiding citizens who professed the true Christian doctrine according to the Holy Scriptures, de Brès prepared this confession in the year 1561. In the following year a copy was sent to King Philip II, together with an address in which the petitioners declared that they were ready to obey the government in all lawful things, but that they would "offer their backs to stripes, their tongues to knives, their mouths to gags, and their whole bodies to the fire," rather than deny the truth expressed in this confession.

Although the immediate purpose of securing freedom from persecution was not attained, and de Brès himself fell as one of the many thousands who sealed their faith with their lives, his work has endured and will continue to endure. In its composition the author availed himself to some extent of a confession of the Reformed churches in France, written chiefly by John Calvin, published two years earlier. The work of de Brès, however, is not a mere revision of Calvin's work, but an independent composition. In 1566 the text of this confession was revised at a synod held at Antwerp. In the Netherlands it was at once gladly received by the churches, and it was adopted by national synods held during the last three decades of the sixteenth century. The text, not the contents, was revised again at the Synod of Dort in 1618-19 and adopted as one of the doctrinal standards to which all office-bearers in the Reformed churches were required to subscribe. The confession is recognized as one of the best official summaries of Reformed doctrine.

The text of Article 36 is presented in two forms in this edition because the Christian Reformed Church in 1938 and 1985 decided to revise it from the original text in order to set forth what it judged to be a more biblical statement on the relationship between church and state, and to eliminate language that denounced "Anabaptists, other anarchists . . ." and so on. The Reformed Church in America has not made any amendments to the Belgic Confession. However, when the Reformed Church in America adopted the Belgic Confession in 1792 as one of the three confessional Standards of Unity, it also adopted the Explanatory Articles that reconciled the statements in the three standards and the Church Order of Dort with the situation in which it existed in the newly independent United States of America. With regard to Article 36 dealing with the relation of church and state, it stated that "whatever relates to the immediate authority and interposition of the Magistrate in the government of the Church, and which is introduced more or less into all the national establishments in Europe, is entirely omitted in the constitution now published." With regard to the harsh words about Anabaptists and others in Article 36, the RCA stated that "in publishing the Articles of Faith, the Church determined to abide by the words adopted in the Synod of Dordrecht, as most expressive of what she believes to be truth; in consequence of which, the terms alluded to could not be avoided. But she openly and candidly declares that she by no means thereby intended to refer to any denomination of Christians at present known, and would be grieved at giving offence, or unnecessarily hurting the feelings of any person."

Article 1: The Only God

We all believe in our hearts
and confess with our mouths
that there is a single
and simple
spiritual being,
whom we call God—

    eternal,
    incomprehensible,
    invisible,
    unchangeable,
    infinite,
    almighty;
    completely wise,
    just,
    and good,
    and the overflowing source
       of all good.

Article 2: The Means by Which We Know God

We know God by two means:

First, by the creation, preservation, and government
of the universe,
since that universe is before our eyes
like a beautiful book
    in which all creatures,
    great and small,
    are as letters
    to make us ponder
    the invisible things of God:
        God's eternal power and divinity,
        as the apostle Paul says in Romans 1:20.

All these things are enough to convict humans
and to leave them without excuse.

Second, God makes himself known to us more clearly
by his holy and divine Word,
as much as we need in this life,
    for God's glory
    and for our salvation.

Article 3: The Written Word of God
We confess that this Word of God
was not sent nor delivered "by human will,"
but that "men and women moved by the Holy Spirit
spoke from God,"
    as Peter says.[1]

Afterward our God—
    with special care
    for us and our salvation—
commanded his servants, the prophets and apostles,
to commit this revealed Word to writing.
God, with his own finger,
wrote the two tables of the law.

Therefore we call such writings
holy and divine Scriptures.

[1] 2 Pet. 1:21

Article 4: The Canonical Books
We include in the Holy Scripture the two volumes
of the Old and New Testaments.
They are canonical books
with which there can be no quarrel at all.

In the church of God the list is as follows:
In the Old Testament,
    the five books of Moses—
        Genesis, Exodus, Leviticus, Numbers, Deuteronomy;
    the books of Joshua, Judges, and Ruth;
    the two books of Samuel, and two of Kings;
    the two books of Chronicles, called Paralipomenon;
    the first book of Ezra; Nehemiah, Esther, Job;
    the Psalms of David;
    the three books of Solomon—
        Proverbs, Ecclesiastes, and the Song;
    the four major prophets—
        Isaiah, Jeremiah*, Ezekiel, Daniel;

and then the other twelve minor prophets—
    Hosea, Joel, Amos, Obadiah,
    Jonah, Micah, Nahum, Habakkuk,
    Zephaniah, Haggai, Zechariah, Malachi.
In the New Testament,
    the four gospels—
    Matthew, Mark, Luke, and John;
    the Acts of the Apostles;
    the fourteen letters of Paul—
        to the Romans;
        the two letters to the Corinthians;
        to the Galatians, Ephesians, Philippians, and Colossians;
        the two letters to the Thessalonians;
        the two letters to Timothy;
        to Titus, Philemon, and to the Hebrews;
    the seven letters of the other apostles—
        one of James;
        two of Peter;
        three of John;
        one of Jude;
    and the Revelation of the apostle John.

* "Jeremiah" here includes the Book of Lamentations as well as the Book of Jeremiah.

Article 5: The Authority of Scripture
We receive all these books
and these only
as holy and canonical,
for the regulating, founding, and establishing
of our faith.

And we believe
without a doubt
all things contained in them—
    not so much because the church
    receives and approves them as such
    but above all because the Holy Spirit
    testifies in our hearts
    that they are from God,
    and also because they
    prove themselves
    to be from God.

    For even the blind themselves are able to see
    that the things predicted in them
    do happen.

Article 6: The Difference Between Canonical and Apocryphal Books

We distinguish between these holy books
and the apocryphal ones,
 which are the third and fourth books of Esdras;
 the books of Tobit, Judith, Wisdom, Jesus Sirach, Baruch;
 what was added to the Story of Esther;
 the Song of the Three Children in the Furnace;
 the Story of Susannah;
 the Story of Bel and the Dragon;
 the Prayer of Manasseh;
 and the two books of Maccabees.

The church may certainly read these books
and learn from them
as far as they agree with the canonical books.
But they do not have such power and virtue
that one could confirm
from their testimony
any point of faith or of the Christian religion.
Much less can they detract
from the authority
of the other holy books.

Article 7: The Sufficiency of Scripture

We believe
that this Holy Scripture contains
the will of God completely
and that everything one must believe
to be saved
is sufficiently taught in it.

For since the entire manner of service
which God requires of us
is described in it at great length,
no one—
 even an apostle
 or an angel from heaven,
 as Paul says—[2]
ought to teach other than
what the Holy Scriptures have
already taught us.

For since it is forbidden
to add to the Word of God,
or take anything away from it,[3]
it is plainly demonstrated
that the teaching is perfect
and complete in all respects.

Therefore we must not consider human writings—
    no matter how holy their authors may have been—
equal to the divine writings;
nor may we put custom,
nor the majority,
nor age,
nor the passage of times or persons,
nor councils, decrees, or official decisions
above the truth of God,
    for truth is above everything else.

For all human beings are liars by nature
and more vain than vanity itself.

Therefore we reject with all our hearts
everything that does not agree
with this infallible rule,
    as we are taught to do by the apostles
    when they say,
        "Test the spirits
        to see whether they are from God,"[4]
    and also,
    "Do not receive into the house
    or welcome anyone
    who comes to you
    and does not bring this teaching."[5]

[2] Gal. 1:8
[3] Deut. 12:32; Rev. 22:18-19
[4] 1 John 4:1
[5] 2 John 10

Article 8: The Trinity

In keeping with this truth and Word of God
we believe in one God,
who is one single essence,
in whom there are three persons,
really, truly, and eternally distinct
according to their incommunicable properties—
    namely,
        Father,
        Son,
        and Holy Spirit.
The Father
    is the cause,
    origin,
    and source of all things,
        visible as well as invisible.

The Son
    is the Word,
    the Wisdom,
    and the image
        of the Father.

The Holy Spirit
    is the eternal power
    and might,
        proceeding from the Father and the Son.

Nevertheless,
this distinction does not divide God into three,
    since Scripture teaches us
    that the Father, the Son, and the Holy Spirit
    each has a distinct subsistence
    distinguished by characteristics—
    yet in such a way
    that these three persons are
    only one God.

It is evident then
that the Father is not the Son
and that the Son is not the Father,
and that likewise the Holy Spirit is
neither the Father nor the Son.

Nevertheless,
these persons,
thus distinct,
are neither divided
nor fused or mixed together.

For the Father did not take on flesh,
nor did the Spirit,
but only the Son.

The Father was never
without the Son,
nor without the Holy Spirit,
since all these are equal from eternity,
in one and the same essence.

There is neither a first nor a last,
for all three are one
in truth and power,
in goodness and mercy.

Article 9: The Scriptural Witness on the Trinity
All these things we know
from the testimonies of Holy Scripture
as well as from the effects of the persons,
especially from those we feel within ourselves.

The testimonies of the Holy Scriptures,
which teach us to believe in this Holy Trinity,
are written in many places of the Old Testament,
which need not be enumerated
but only chosen with discretion.

In the book of Genesis God says,
"Let us make humankind in our image,
according to our likeness."
So "God created humankind in his image"—
indeed, "male and female he created them."[6]
"See, the man has become like one of us."[7]

It appears from this
that there is a plurality of persons
within the Deity,
when God says,
"Let us make humankind in our image"—
and afterward God indicates the unity
in saying,
"God created."

It is true that God does not say here
how many persons there are—
but what is somewhat obscure to us
in the Old Testament
is very clear in the New.

For when our Lord was baptized in the Jordan,
the voice of the Father was heard saying,
    "This is my Son, the Beloved;"[8]
the Son was seen in the water;
and the Holy Spirit appeared in the form of a dove.

So, in the baptism of all believers
this form was prescribed by Christ:
    Baptize all people "in the name
    of the Father
    and of the Son
    and of the Holy Spirit."[9]

In the Gospel according to Luke
the angel Gabriel says to Mary,
the mother of our Lord:

    "The Holy Spirit will come upon you,
    and the power of the Most High will overshadow you;
    therefore the child to be born will be holy;
    he will be called Son of God."[10]

And in another place it says:
    "The grace of the Lord Jesus Christ,
    the love of God,
    and the communion of the Holy Spirit
    be with all of you."[11]

    ["There are three that testify in heaven,
    the Father, the Word, and the Holy Spirit,
    and these three are one."][12]

In all these passages we are fully taught
that there are three persons
in the one and only divine essence.
And although this doctrine surpasses human understanding,
we nevertheless believe it now,
    through the Word,
waiting to know and enjoy it fully
    in heaven.

Furthermore,
we must note the particular works and activities
of these three persons in relation to us.
    The Father is called our Creator,
        by reason of his power.
    The Son is our Savior and Redeemer,
        by his blood.

The Holy Spirit is our Sanctifier,
    by living in our hearts.

This doctrine of the holy Trinity
has always been maintained in the true church,
    from the time of the apostles until the present,
    against Jews, Muslims,
    and certain false Christians and heretics,
        such as Marcion, Mani,
        Praxeas, Sabellius, Paul of Samosata, Arius,
        and others like them,
        who were rightly condemned by the holy fathers.

And so,
in this matter we willingly accept
    the three ecumenical creeds—
    the Apostles', Nicene, and Athanasian—
    as well as what the ancient fathers decided
    in agreement with them.

[6] Gen. 1:26-27
[7] Gen. 3:22
[8] Matt. 3:17
[9] Matt. 28:19
[10] Luke 1:35
[11] 2 Cor. 13:14
[12] 1 John 5:7—following the better Greek texts, the NRSV and other modern translations place this verse in a footnote.

Article 10: The Deity of Christ
We believe that Jesus Christ,
according to his divine nature,
is the only Son of God—
    eternally begotten,
    not made or created,
        for then he would be a creature.

He is one in essence with the Father;
coeternal;
the exact image of the person of the Father
and the "reflection of God's glory,"[13]
    being like the Father in all things.

Jesus Christ is the Son of God
not only from the time he assumed our nature
but from all eternity,
    as the following testimonies teach us
    when they are taken together.

Moses says that God created the world;[14]
and John says that all things were created through the Word,[15]
    which he calls God.
The apostle says that God created the world through the Son.[16]
He also says that God created all things through Jesus Christ.[17]

And so it must follow
that the one who is called God, the Word, the Son, and Jesus Christ
already existed before creating all things.
Therefore the prophet Micah says
that Christ's origin is "from ancient days."[18]
And the apostle says
that the Son has "neither beginning of days
    nor end of life."[19]

So then,
he is the true eternal God,
the Almighty,
whom we invoke,
worship,
and serve.

[13] Col. 1:15; Heb. 1:3
[14] Gen. 1:1
[15] John 1:3
[16] Heb. 1:2
[17] Col. 1:16
[18] Mic. 5:2
[19] Heb. 7:3

Article 11: The Deity of the Holy Spirit
We believe and confess also
that the Holy Spirit proceeds eternally
from the Father and the Son—
    neither made,
    nor created,
    nor begotten,
    but only proceeding
    from the two of them.

In regard to order,
the Spirit is the third person of the Trinity—
    of one and the same essence,
    and majesty,
    and glory,
    with the Father and the Son,
being true and eternal God,
    as the Holy Scriptures teach us.

Article 12: The Creation of All Things

We believe that the Father,
when it seemed good to him,
created heaven and earth and all other creatures
from nothing,
by the Word—
    that is to say,
    by the Son.

God has given all creatures
their being, form, and appearance
and their various functions
    for serving their Creator.

Even now
God also sustains and governs them all,
according to his eternal providence
and by his infinite power,
    that they may serve humanity,
    in order that humanity may serve God.

God has also created the angels good,
that they might be messengers of God
and serve the elect.

    Some of them have fallen
        from the excellence in which God created them
        into eternal perdition;
    and the others have persisted and remained
        in their original state,
        by the grace of God.
    The devils and evil spirits are so corrupt
    that they are enemies of God
    and of everything good.
    They lie in wait for the church
    and every member of it
    like thieves,
        with all their power,
    to destroy and spoil everything
        by their deceptions.

    So then,
    by their own wickedness
    they are condemned to everlasting damnation,
        daily awaiting their torments.

For that reason
we detest the error of the Sadducees,
    who deny that there are spirits and angels,
and also the error of the Manicheans,
    who say that the devils originated by themselves,
    being evil by nature,
        without having been corrupted.

Article 13: The Doctrine of God's Providence
We believe that this good God,
    after creating all things,
did not abandon them to chance or fortune
but leads and governs them
    according to his holy will,
in such a way that nothing happens in this world
without God's orderly arrangement.

Yet God is not the author of,
and cannot be charged with,
the sin that occurs.
For God's power and goodness
are so great and incomprehensible
that God arranges and does his works very well and justly
even when the devils and the wicked act unjustly.

We do not wish to inquire
    with undue curiosity
into what God does that surpasses human understanding
    and is beyond our ability to comprehend.
But in all humility and reverence
we adore the just judgments of God,
which are hidden from us,
    being content to be Christ's disciples,
        so as to learn only what God shows us in the Word,
            without going beyond those limits.

This doctrine gives us unspeakable comfort
since it teaches us
that nothing can happen to us by chance
but only by the arrangement of our gracious
heavenly Father,
who watches over us with fatherly care,
sustaining all creatures under his lordship,
so that not one of the hairs on our heads
(for they are all numbered)
nor even a little bird
can fall to the ground
without the will of our Father.[20]

In this thought we rest,
knowing that God holds in check
the devils and all our enemies,
    who cannot hurt us
    without divine permission and will.

For that reason we reject
the damnable error of the Epicureans,
    who say that God does not get involved in anything
    and leaves everything to chance.

[20] Matt. 10:29-30

Article 14: The Creation and Fall of Humanity
We believe
that God created human beings from the dust of the earth
and made and formed them in his image and likeness—
    good, just, and holy;
    able by their will to conform
    in all things
    to the will of God.

But when they were in honor
they did not understand it[21]
and did not recognize their excellence.
But they subjected themselves willingly to sin
and consequently to death and the curse,
    lending their ear to the word of the devil.

For they transgressed the commandment of life,
    which they had received,
and by their sin they separated themselves from God,
    who was their true life,
having corrupted their entire nature.

So they made themselves guilty
and subject to physical and spiritual death,
    having become wicked,
    perverse,
    and corrupt in all their ways.

They lost all their excellent gifts
    which they had received from God,
and retained none of them
except for small traces
    which are enough to make them
    inexcusable.

Moreover, all the light in us is turned to darkness,
as the Scripture teaches us:
  "The light shines in the darkness,
  and the darkness did not overcome it."[22]
Here John calls the human race "darkness."

Therefore we reject everything taught to the contrary
concerning human free will,
since humans are nothing but the slaves of sin
and cannot do a thing
unless it is given them from heaven.[23]

For who can boast of being able
to do anything good by oneself,
since Christ says,
  "No one can come to me
  unless drawn by the Father who sent me"?[24]

Who can glory in their own will
  when they understand that "the mind that is set on the flesh
  is hostile to God"?[25]
Who can speak of their own knowledge
  in view of the fact that "those who are unspiritual
  do not receive the gifts of God's Spirit"?[26]

In short,
who can produce a single thought,
  knowing that we are not able to think a thing
  about ourselves,
  by ourselves,
  but that "our competence is from God"?[27]

And therefore,
what the apostle says
ought rightly to stand fixed and firm:
  God works within us
  both to will and to do
  according to his good pleasure.[28]

For there is no understanding nor will
conforming to God's understanding and will
apart from Christ's involvement,
    as he teaches us when he says,
    "Apart from me you can do nothing."[29]

[21] Ps. 49:20
[22] John 1:5
[23] John 3:27
[24] John 6:44
[25] Rom. 8:7
[26] 1 Cor. 2:14
[27] 2 Cor. 3:5
[28] Phil. 2:13
[29] John 15:5

Article 15: The Doctrine of Original Sin
We believe
that by the disobedience of Adam
original sin has been spread
through the whole human race.[30]

It is a corruption of the whole human nature—
an inherited depravity which even infects small infants
    in their mother's womb,
and the root which produces in humanity
    every sort of sin.
It is therefore so vile and enormous in God's sight
that it is enough to condemn the human race,
and it is not abolished
    or wholly uprooted
    even by baptism,
        seeing that sin constantly boils forth
        as though from a contaminated spring.

Nevertheless,
it is not imputed to God's children
for their condemnation
but is forgiven
by his grace and mercy—
    not to put them to sleep
    but so that the awareness of this corruption
    might often make believers groan
    as they long to be set free
    from the body of this death.[31]

Therefore we reject the error of the Pelagians
who say that this sin is nothing else than a matter of imitation.

[30] Rom. 5:12-13
[31] Rom. 7:24

Article 16: The Doctrine of Election

We believe that—
    all Adam's descendants having thus fallen
    into perdition and ruin
    by the sin of Adam—
God showed himself to be as he is:
merciful and just.

God is merciful
in withdrawing and saving from this perdition those who,
    in the eternal and unchangeable divine counsel,
have been elected and chosen in Jesus Christ our Lord
    by his pure goodness,
    without any consideration of their works.

God is just
in leaving the others in their ruin and fall
into which they plunged themselves.

Article 17: The Recovery of Fallen Humanity

We believe that our good God,
by marvelous divine wisdom and goodness,
    seeing that Adam and Eve had plunged themselves in this manner
    into both physical and spiritual death
    and made themselves completely miserable,
set out to find them,
though they,
    trembling all over,
were fleeing from God.

And God comforted them,
promising to give them his Son,
    born of a woman,[32]
to crush the head of the serpent,[33]
and to make them blessed.

[32] Gal. 4:4
[33] Gen. 3:15

Article 18: The Incarnation

So then we confess
that God fulfilled the promise
    made to the early fathers and mothers
    by the mouth of the holy prophets
when he sent the only and eternal Son of God
into the world
at the time appointed.

The Son took the "form of a slave"
and was made in "human form,"[34]
    truly assuming a real human nature,
    with all its weaknesses,
    except for sin;
    being conceived in the womb of the blessed virgin Mary
    by the power of the Holy Spirit,
    without male participation.

And Christ not only assumed human nature
    as far as the body is concerned
but also a real human soul,
    in order to be a real human being.
For since the soul had been lost as well as the body,
Christ had to assume them both
to save them both together.

Therefore we confess
    (against the heresy of the Anabaptists
    who deny that Christ assumed
    human flesh from his mother)
that Christ shared the very flesh and blood of children;[35]
being the fruit of the loins of David according to the flesh,[36]
descended from David according to the flesh;[37]
the fruit of the womb of the virgin Mary;[38]
born of a woman;[39]
the seed of David;[40]
the root of Jesse;[41]
descended from Judah,[42]
    having descended from the Jews according to the flesh;
descended from Abraham—
    having assumed descent from Abraham and Sarah,
    and was made like his brothers and sisters,
        yet without sin.[43]

In this way Christ is truly our Immanuel—
    that is: "God with us."[44]

[34] Phil. 2:7
[35] Heb. 2:14
[36] Acts 2:30
[37] Rom. 1:3
[38] Luke 1:42
[39] Gal. 4:4
[40] 2 Tim. 2:8
[41] Rom. 15:12
[42] Heb. 7:14
[43] Heb. 2:17; 4:15
[44] Matt. 1:23

Article 19: The Two Natures of Christ

We believe that by being thus conceived
the person of the Son has been inseparably united
and joined together
with human nature,
    in such a way that there are not two Sons of God,
    nor two persons,
    but two natures united in a single person,
    with each nature retaining its own distinct properties.

Thus his divine nature has always remained uncreated,
    without beginning of days or end of life,[45]
    filling heaven and earth.

Christ's human nature has not lost its properties
but continues to have those of a creature—
    it has a beginning of days;
    it is of a finite nature
    and retains all that belongs to a real body.
    And even though he,
    by his resurrection,
    gave it immortality,
    that nonetheless did not change
    the reality of his human nature;
    for our salvation and resurrection
    depend also on the reality of his body.

But these two natures
are so united together in one person
that they are not even separated by his death.

So then,
what he committed to his Father when he died
was a real human spirit which left his body.
But meanwhile his divine nature remained
united with his human nature
    even when he was lying in the grave;
and his deity never ceased to be in him,
    just as it was in him when he was a little child,
    though for a while it did not so reveal itself.

These are the reasons why we confess him
to be true God and truly human—
   true God in order to conquer death
      by his power,
   and truly human that he might die for us
      in the weakness of his flesh.

[45] Heb. 7:3

Article 20: The Justice and Mercy of God in Christ

We believe that God—
   who is perfectly merciful
   and also very just—
sent the Son to assume the nature
in which the disobedience had been committed,
   in order to bear in it the punishment of sin
   by his most bitter passion and death.

So God made known his justice toward his Son,
   who was charged with our sin,
and he poured out his goodness and mercy on us,
   who are guilty and worthy of damnation,
giving to us his Son to die,
   by a most perfect love,
and raising him to life
   for our justification,
      in order that by him
      we might have immortality
      and eternal life.

Article 21: The Atonement

We believe
that Jesus Christ is a high priest forever
according to the order of Melchizedek—
   made such by an oath—
and that he presented himself
in our name
before his Father,
to appease his Father's wrath
with full satisfaction
   by offering himself
      on the tree of the cross
   and pouring out his precious blood
      for the cleansing of our sins,
      as the prophets had predicted.

For it is written
that "the punishment that made us whole"
was placed on the Son of God
and that "by his bruises we are healed."
He was "like a lamb that is led to the slaughter";
he was "numbered with the transgressors"[46]
and condemned as a criminal by Pontius Pilate,
    though Pilate had declared
    that he was innocent.

So he paid back
what he had not stolen,[47]
and he suffered—
    "the righteous for the unrighteous,"[48]
    in both his body and his soul—
in such a way that
when he sensed the horrible punishment
required by our sins
"his sweat became like great drops of blood
falling down on the ground."[49]
He cried, "My God, my God,
why have you forsaken me?"[50]

And he endured all this
for the forgiveness of our sins.

Therefore we rightly say with Paul that
we know nothing "except Jesus Christ, and him crucified";[51]
we "regard everything as loss
because of the surpassing value
of knowing Christ Jesus [our] Lord."[52]
We find all comforts in his wounds
and have no need to seek or invent any other means
to reconcile ourselves with God
than this one and only sacrifice,
once made,
which renders believers perfect
forever.

This is also why
the angel of God called him Jesus—
that is, "Savior"—
　　because he would save his people
　　from their sins.[53]

[46] Isa. 53:4-12
[47] Ps. 69:4
[48] 1 Pet. 3:18
[49] Luke 22:44
[50] Matt. 27:46
[51] 1 Cor. 2:2
[52] Phil. 3:8
[53] Matt. 1:21

Article 22: The Righteousness of Faith
We believe that
for us to acquire the true knowledge of this great mystery
the Holy Spirit kindles in our hearts a true faith
that embraces Jesus Christ,
　　with all his merits,
and makes him its own,
and no longer looks for anything
　　apart from him.

For it must necessarily follow
that either all that is required for our salvation
is not in Christ or,
if all is in him,
then those who have Christ by faith
have his salvation entirely.

Therefore,
to say that Christ is not enough
but that something else is needed as well
is a most enormous blasphemy against God—
　　for it then would follow
　　that Jesus Christ is only half a Savior.
And therefore we justly say with Paul
that we are justified "by faith alone"
or "by faith apart from works."[54]

However,
we do not mean,
properly speaking,
that it is faith itself that justifies us—
　　for faith is only the instrument
　　by which we embrace Christ,
　　our righteousness.

But Jesus Christ is our righteousness
in making available to us all his merits
and all the holy works he has done
for us and in our place.
And faith is the instrument
that keeps us in communion with him
and with all his benefits.

When those benefits are made ours,
they are more than enough to absolve us
of our sins.

54 Rom. 3:28

Article 23: The Justification of Sinners
We believe
that our blessedness lies in the forgiveness of our sins
because of Jesus Christ,
and that in it our righteousness before God is contained,
as David and Paul teach us
when they declare those people blessed
to whom God grants righteousness
apart from works.[55]

And the same apostle says
that we are "justified by his grace as a gift,
through the redemption that is in Christ Jesus."[56]
And therefore we cling to this foundation,
which is firm forever,
giving all glory to God,
humbling ourselves,
and recognizing ourselves as we are;
not claiming a thing for ourselves or our merits
and leaning and resting
on the sole obedience of Christ crucified,
which is ours when we believe in him.

That is enough to cover all our sins
and to make us confident,
freeing the conscience from the fear, dread, and terror
of God's approach,
without doing what our first parents, Adam and Eve, did,
who trembled as they tried to cover themselves
with fig leaves.

In fact,
if we had to appear before God relying—
    no matter how little—
on ourselves or some other creature,
then, alas, we would be swallowed up.

Therefore everyone must say with David:
"[Lord,] do not enter into judgment with your servant,
    for no one living is righteous before you."[57]

[55] Ps. 32:1; Rom. 4:6
[56] Rom. 3:24
[57] Ps. 143:2

Article 24: The Sanctification of Sinners

We believe that this true faith,
    produced in us by the hearing of God's Word
    and by the work of the Holy Spirit,
regenerates us and makes us new creatures,[58]
    causing us to live a new life[59]
    and freeing us from the slavery of sin.

Therefore,
far from making people cold
toward living in a pious and holy way,
this justifying faith,
quite to the contrary,
so works within them that
    apart from it
they will never do a thing out of love for God
but only out of love for themselves
and fear of being condemned.

So then, it is impossible
for this holy faith to be unfruitful in a human being,
seeing that we do not speak of an empty faith
but of what Scripture calls
"faith working through love,"[60]
    which moves people to do by themselves
    the works that God has commanded
        in the Word.

These works,
    proceeding from the good root of faith,
are good and acceptable to God,
    since they are all sanctified by God's grace.

Yet they do not count toward our justification—
    for by faith in Christ we are justified,
    even before we do good works.
        Otherwise they could not be good,
        any more than the fruit of a tree could be good
        if the tree is not good in the first place.

So then, we do good works,
but not for merit—
    for what would we merit?
Rather, we are indebted to God for the good works we do,
    and not God to us,
since God "is at work in [us], enabling [us] both
    to will and to work for his good pleasure"[61] —
thus keeping in mind what is written:
    "When you have done all that you were ordered to do,
    say, 'We are worthless slaves;
    we have done only what we ought to have done.'"[62]

Yet we do not wish to deny
that God rewards good works—
but it is by grace
that God crowns these gifts.

Moreover,
although we do good works
we do not base our salvation on them;
    for we cannot do any work
    that is not defiled by our flesh
    and also worthy of punishment.
And even if we could point to one,
    memory of a single sin is enough
    for God to reject that work.

So we would always be in doubt,
    tossed back and forth
    without any certainty,
and our poor consciences would be tormented constantly
    if they did not rest on the merit
    of the suffering and death of our Savior.

[58] 2 Cor. 5:17
[59] Rom. 6:4
[60] Gal. 5:6
[61] Phil. 2:13
[62] Luke 17:10

Article 25: The Fulfillment of the Law

We believe
that the ceremonies and symbols of the law have ended
    with the coming of Christ,
and that all foreshadowings have come to an end,
so that the use of them ought to be abolished
    among Christians.
Yet the truth and substance of these things
remain for us in Jesus Christ,
    in whom they have been fulfilled.

Nevertheless,
we continue to use the witnesses
drawn from the law and prophets
    to confirm us in the gospel
    and to regulate our lives with full integrity
      for the glory of God,
      according to the will of God.

Article 26: The Intercession of Christ

We believe that we have no access to God
except through the one and only Mediator and Intercessor,
"Jesus Christ the righteous,"[63]
who
therefore was made human,
uniting together the divine and human natures,
so that we human beings might have access to the divine Majesty.
Otherwise we would have no access.

But this Mediator,
    whom the Father has appointed between himself and us,
ought not terrify us by his greatness,
    so that we have to look for another one,
    according to our fancy.
For neither in heaven nor among the creatures on earth
is there anyone who loves us
more than Jesus Christ does.
    Although he was "in the form of God,"
    Christ nevertheless "emptied himself,"
    taking "human form" and "the form of a slave" for us;[64]
    and he made himself "like his brothers and sisters
      in every respect."[65]

Suppose we had to find another intercessor.
Who would love us more than he who gave his life for us,
even though "we were enemies"?[66]
And suppose we had to find one who has prestige and power.
Who has as much of these as he who is seated
at the right hand of the Father,[67]
and who has "all authority
in heaven and on earth"?[68]
And who will be heard more readily
than God's own dearly beloved Son?

So, the practice of honoring the saints as intercessors
in fact dishonors them
because of its misplaced faith.
That was something the saints never did nor asked for,
but which in keeping with their duty,
as appears from their writings,
they consistently refused.

We should not plead here
that we are unworthy—
for it is not a question of offering our prayers
on the basis of our own dignity
but only on the basis of the excellence and dignity
of Jesus Christ,
whose righteousness is ours by faith.

Since the apostle for good reason
wants us to get rid of this foolish fear—
or rather, this unbelief—
he says to us that Jesus Christ
was made like "his brothers and sisters in every respect,
so that he might be a merciful and faithful high priest"
to purify the sins of the people.[69]
For since he suffered,
being tempted,
he is also able to help those
who are tempted.[70]

And further,
to encourage us more
to approach him
he says,
"Since, then, we have a great high priest
who has passed through the heavens,
Jesus, the Son of God,
let us hold fast to our confession.
For we do not have a high priest

who is unable to sympathize with our weaknesses,
but we have one who in every respect has been tested
as we are,
yet without sin.
Let us therefore approach
the throne of grace
with boldness,
so that we may receive mercy
and find grace
to help in time of need."[71]

The same apostle says that
we "have confidence to enter the sanctuary
by the blood of Jesus."
"Let us approach with a true heart
in full assurance of faith...."[72]

Likewise,
Christ "holds his priesthood permanently....
Consequently, he is able for all time to save
those who approach God through him,
since he always lives
to make intercession for them."[73]

What more do we need?
For Christ himself declares:
"I am the way, and the truth, and the life.
No one comes to the Father
except through me."[74]
Why should we seek
another intercessor?

Since it has pleased God
to give us the Son as our Intercessor.
let us not leave him for another—
    or rather seek, without ever finding.
For, when giving Christ to us,
God knew well that we were sinners.

Therefore,
in following the command of Christ
we call on the heavenly Father
through Christ,
our only Mediator,
as we are taught by the Lord's Prayer,
being assured that we shall obtain
all we ask of the Father
in his name.

[63] 1 John 2:1
[64] Phil. 2:6-8
[65] Heb. 2:17
[66] Rom. 5:10
[67] Rom. 8:34; Heb. 1:3
[68] Matt. 28:18
[69] Heb. 2:17
[70] Heb. 2:18
[71] Heb. 4:14-16
[72] Heb. 10:19, 22
[73] Heb. 7:24-25
[74] John 14:6

Article 27: The Holy Catholic Church

We believe and confess
one single catholic or universal church—
a holy congregation and gathering
of true Christian believers,
awaiting their entire salvation in Jesus Christ,
being washed by his blood,
and sanctified and sealed by the Holy Spirit.

This church has existed from the beginning of the world
and will last until the end,
as appears from the fact
that Christ is eternal King
who cannot be without subjects.

And this holy church is preserved by God
against the rage of the whole world,
even though for a time
it may appear very small
to human eyes—
as though it were snuffed out.

For example,
during the very dangerous time of Ahab
the Lord preserved for himself seven thousand
who did not bend their knees to Baal.[75]

And so this holy church
is not confined,
bound,
or limited to a certain place or certain people.

But it is spread and dispersed
throughout the entire world,
    though still joined and united
        in heart and will,
        in one and the same Spirit,
        by the power of faith.

[75] 1 Kings 19:18

Article 28: The Obligations of Church Members
We believe that
    since this holy assembly and congregation
    is the gathering of those who are saved
    and there is no salvation apart from it,
people ought not to withdraw from it,
    content to be by themselves,
    regardless of their status or condition.

But all people are obliged
to join and unite with it,
keeping the unity of the church
    by submitting to its instruction and discipline,
    by bending their necks under the yoke of Jesus Christ,
    and by serving to build up one another,
according to the gifts God has given them
as members of each other
in the same body.

And to preserve this unity more effectively,
it is the duty of all believers,
    according to God's Word,
to separate themselves
from those who do not belong to the church,
    in order to join this assembly
    wherever God has established it,
        even if civil authorities and royal decrees forbid
        and death and physical punishment result.

And so,
all who withdraw from the church
or do not join it
act contrary to God's ordinance.

Article 29: The Marks of the True Church

We believe that we ought to discern
    diligently and very carefully,
    by the Word of God,
what is the true church—
    for all sects in the world today
    claim for themselves the name of "the church."

We are not speaking here of the company of hypocrites
who are mixed among the good in the church
and who nonetheless are not part of it,
even though they are physically there.
But we are speaking of distinguishing
the body and fellowship of the true church
from all sects that call themselves "the church."

The true church can be recognized
if it has the following marks:
    The church engages in the pure preaching
        of the gospel;
    it makes use of the pure administration of the sacraments
        as Christ instituted them;
    it practices church discipline
        for correcting faults.

In short, it governs itself
according to the pure Word of God,
    rejecting all things contrary to it
    and holding Jesus Christ as the only Head.
By these marks one can be assured
of recognizing the true church—
    and no one ought to be separated from it.

As for those who can belong to the church,
we can recognize them by the distinguishing marks of Christians:
    namely by faith,
    and by their fleeing from sin and pursuing righteousness,
        once they have received the one and only Savior,
        Jesus Christ.

They love the true God and their neighbors,
    without turning to the right or left,
and they crucify the flesh and its works.

Though great weakness remains in them,
they fight against it
by the Spirit
all the days of their lives,

appealing constantly
to the blood, suffering, death, and obedience of the Lord Jesus,
    in whom they have forgiveness of their sins,
    through faith in him.

As for the false church,
it assigns more authority to itself and its ordinances
    than to the Word of God;
it does not want to subject itself
    to the yoke of Christ;
it does not administer the sacraments
    as Christ commanded in his Word;
it rather adds to them or subtracts from them
    as it pleases;
it bases itself on humans,
    more than on Jesus Christ;
it persecutes those
    who live holy lives according to the Word of God
    and who rebuke it for its faults, greed, and idolatry.

These two churches
are easy to recognize
and thus to distinguish
from each other.

Article 30: The Government of the Church

We believe that this true church
ought to be governed according to the spiritual order
that our Lord has taught us in his Word.
    There should be ministers or pastors
        to preach the Word of God
        and administer the sacraments.
    There should also be elders and deacons,
        along with the pastors,
        to make up the council of the church.

By this means
true religion is preserved;
true doctrine is able to take its course;
and evil people are corrected spiritually and held in check,
    so that also the poor
    and all the afflicted
    may be helped and comforted
    according to their need.

By this means
everything will be done well
and in good order
in the church,
    when such persons are elected
    who are faithful
    and are chosen according to the rule
    that Paul gave to Timothy.[76]

[76] 1 Tim. 3

Article 31: The Officers of the Church

We believe that
ministers of the Word of God, elders, and deacons
ought to be chosen to their offices
by a legitimate election of the church,
with prayer in the name of the Lord,
and in good order,
    as the Word of God teaches.

So all must be careful
not to push themselves forward improperly,
but must wait for God's call,
    so that they may be assured of their calling
    and be certain that they are
    chosen by the Lord.

As for the ministers of the Word,
they all have the same power and authority,
    no matter where they may be,
since they are all servants of Jesus Christ,
    the only universal bishop,
    and the only head of the church.

Moreover,
to keep God's holy order
from being violated or despised,
we say that everyone ought,
as much as possible,
to hold the ministers of the Word and elders of the church
in special esteem,
    because of the work they do,
and be at peace with them,
    without grumbling, quarreling, or fighting.

Article 32: The Order and Discipline of the Church
We also believe that
although it is useful and good
for those who govern the churches
to establish and set up
a certain order among themselves
for maintaining the body of the church,
they ought always to guard against deviating
from what Christ,
our only Master,
has ordained
for us.

Therefore we reject all human innovations
and all laws imposed on us,
in our worship of God,
which bind and force our consciences
in any way.

So we accept only what is proper
to maintain harmony and unity
and to keep all in obedience
to God.

To that end excommunication,
with all it involves,
according to the Word of God,
is required.

Article 33: The Sacraments
We believe that our good God,
mindful of our crudeness and weakness,
has ordained sacraments for us
    to seal his promises in us,
      to pledge good will and grace toward us,
      and also to nourish and sustain our faith.

God has added these to the Word of the gospel
to represent better to our external senses
both what God enables us to understand by the Word
and what he does inwardly in our hearts,
    confirming in us
    the salvation he imparts to us.

For they are visible signs and seals
of something internal and invisible,
    by means of which God works in us
    through the power of the Holy Spirit.
So they are not empty and hollow signs
to fool and deceive us,
    for their truth is Jesus Christ,
    without whom they would be nothing.

Moreover,
we are satisfied with the number of sacraments
that Christ our Master has ordained for us.
There are only two:
    the sacrament of baptism
    and the Holy Supper of Jesus Christ.

Article 34: The Sacrament of Baptism

We believe and confess that Jesus Christ,
in whom the law is fulfilled,
has by his shed blood
put an end to every other shedding of blood,
    which anyone might do or wish to do
    in order to atone or satisfy for sins.

Having abolished circumcision,
which was done with blood,
Christ established in its place
the sacrament of baptism.

    By it we are received into God's church
        and set apart from all other people and alien religions,
    that we may wholly belong to him
        whose mark and sign we bear.
    Baptism also witnesses to us
    that God, being our gracious Father,
        will be our God forever.

Therefore Christ has commanded
that all those who belong to him
be baptized with pure water
    "in the name of the Father
    and of the Son
    and of the Holy Spirit."[77]

In this way God signifies to us
that just as water washes away the dirt of the body
when it is poured on us
and also is seen on the bodies of those who are baptized
when it is sprinkled on them,
so too the blood of Christ does the same thing internally,
in the soul,
by the Holy Spirit.

It washes and cleanses it from its sins
and transforms us from being the children of wrath
into the children of God.

This does not happen by the physical water
but by the sprinkling of the precious blood of the Son of God,
who is our Red Sea,
through which we must pass
to escape the tyranny of Pharaoh,
who is the devil,
and to enter the spiritual land
of Canaan.

So ministers,
as far as their work is concerned,
give us the sacrament and what is visible,
but our Lord gives what the sacrament signifies—
namely the invisible gifts and graces;
washing, purifying, and cleansing our souls
of all filth and unrighteousness;
renewing our hearts and filling them
with all comfort;
giving us true assurance
of his fatherly goodness;
clothing us with the "new self"
and stripping off the "old self
with its practices."[78]

For this reason we believe that
anyone who aspires to reach eternal life
ought to be baptized only once
without ever repeating it—
for we cannot be born twice.
Yet this baptism is profitable
not only when the water is on us
and when we receive it
but throughout our
entire lives.

For that reason we reject the error of the Anabaptists
   who are not content with a single baptism
      once received
   and also condemn the baptism
      of the children of believers.
   We believe our children ought to be baptized
   and sealed with the sign of the covenant,
      as little children were circumcised in Israel
      on the basis of the same promises
      made to our children.

And truly,
Christ has shed his blood no less
for washing the little children of believers
than he did for adults.

Therefore they ought to receive the sign and sacrament
of what Christ has done for them,
   just as the Lord commanded in the law that
   by offering a lamb for them
   the sacrament of the suffering and death of Christ
   would be granted them
   shortly after their birth.
   This was the sacrament of Jesus Christ.

Furthermore,
baptism does for our children
what circumcision did for the Jewish people.
That is why Paul calls baptism
the "circumcision of Christ."[79]

[77] Matt. 28:19
[78] Col. 3:9-10
[79] Col. 2:11

Article 35: The Sacrament of the Lord's Supper
We believe and confess
that our Savior Jesus Christ
has ordained and instituted the sacrament of the Holy Supper
to nourish and sustain those
who are already regenerated and ingrafted
into his family,
which is his church.

Now those who are born again have two lives in them.
The one is physical and temporal—
   they have it from the moment of their first birth,
   and it is common to all.

The other is spiritual and heavenly,
    and is given them in their second birth—
    it comes through the Word of the gospel
    in the communion of the body of Christ;
    and this life is common to God's elect only.

Thus, to support the physical and earthly life
God has prescribed for us
an appropriate earthly and material bread,
which is as common to all people
as life itself.
But to maintain the spiritual and heavenly life
that belongs to believers,
God has sent a living bread
that came down from heaven:
namely Jesus Christ,
    who nourishes and maintains
    the spiritual life of believers
    when eaten—
    that is, when appropriated
    and received spiritually
    by faith.

To represent to us
this spiritual and heavenly bread
Christ has instituted
an earthly and visible bread as the sacrament of his body
and wine as the sacrament of his blood.
He did this to testify to us that
just as truly as we take and hold the sacrament in our hands
and eat and drink it with our mouths,
    by which our life is then sustained,
so truly we receive into our souls,
    for our spiritual life,
the true body and true blood of Christ,
    our only Savior.
We receive these by faith,
    which is the hand and mouth of our souls.

Now it is certain
that Jesus Christ did not prescribe
his sacraments for us in vain,
since he works in us all he represents

by these holy signs,
    although the manner in which he does it
    goes beyond our understanding
    and is incomprehensible to us,
        just as the operation of God's Spirit
        is hidden and incomprehensible.

Yet we do not go wrong when we say
that what is eaten is Christ's own natural body
and what is drunk is his own blood—
but the manner in which we eat it
is not by the mouth, but by the Spirit
through faith.

In that way Jesus Christ remains always seated
at the right hand of God the Father
in heaven—
but he never refrains on that account
to communicate himself to us
through faith.
This banquet is a spiritual table
at which Christ communicates himself to us
with all his benefits.
At that table he makes us enjoy himself
as much as the merits of his suffering and death,
as he nourishes, strengthens, and comforts
our poor, desolate souls
    by the eating of his flesh,
and relieves and renews them
    by the drinking of his blood.

Moreover,
though the sacraments and what they signify are joined together,
not all receive both of them.
The wicked certainly take the sacrament,
to their condemnation,
but do not receive the truth of the sacrament,
    just as Judas and Simon the Sorcerer both indeed
    received the sacrament,
    but not Christ,
    who was signified by it.
    He is communicated only to believers.

Finally,
with humility and reverence
we receive the holy sacrament
in the gathering of God's people,

as we engage together,
with thanksgiving,
in a holy remembrance
of the death of Christ our Savior,
and as we thus confess
our faith and Christian religion.
Therefore none should come to this table
without examining themselves carefully,
    lest by eating this bread
    and drinking this cup
    they "eat and drink judgment against themselves."[80]

In short,
by the use of this holy sacrament
we are moved to a fervent love
of God and our neighbors.

Therefore we reject
as desecrations of the sacraments
all the muddled ideas and condemnable inventions
that people have added and mixed in with them.
And we say that we should be content with the procedure
that Christ and the apostles have taught us
and speak of these things
as they have spoken of them.

[80] 1 Cor. 11:29

Article 36: The Civil Government
We believe that
because of the depravity of the human race,
our good God has ordained kings, princes, and civil officers.
God wants the world to be governed by laws and policies
so that human lawlessness may be restrained
and that everything may be conducted in good order
among human beings.

For that purpose God has placed the sword
in the hands of the government,
to punish evil people
and protect the good.

[RCA only*
And the government's task is not limited
to caring for and watching over the public domain
but extends also to upholding the sacred ministry,
    with a view to removing and destroying
        all idolatry and false worship of the Antichrist;
    to promoting the kingdom of Jesus Christ;
    and to furthering the preaching of the gospel everywhere;
    to the end that God may be honored and served by everyone,
    as he requires in his Word.]

[CRC only**
And being called in this manner
to contribute to the advancement of a society
that is pleasing to God,
the civil rulers have the task,
    subject to God's law,
of removing every obstacle
    to the preaching of the gospel
    and to every aspect of divine worship.

They should do this
while completely refraining from every tendency
    toward exercising absolute authority,
and while functioning in the sphere entrusted to them,
    with the means belonging to them.

They should do it in order that
    the Word of God may have free course;
    the kingdom of Jesus Christ may make progress;
    and every anti-Christian power may be resisted.]

Moreover everyone,
regardless of status, condition, or rank,
must be subject to the government,
and pay taxes,
and hold its representatives in honor and respect,
and obey them in all things that are not in conflict
    with God's Word,
praying for them
    that the Lord may be willing to lead them
        in all their ways
    and that we may live a peaceful and quiet life
        in all piety and decency.

[RCA only***
And on this matter we reject the Anabaptists, anarchists,
and in general all those who want
to reject the authorities and civil officers
and to subvert justice
    by introducing common ownership of goods
    and corrupting the moral order
        that God has established among human beings.]

* The Reformed Church in America retains the original full text, choosing to recognize that the confession was written within a historical context which may not accurately describe the situation that pertains today.
**Synod 1958 of the Christian Reformed Church replaced the aforementioned paragraph with the following three paragraphs (in brackets).
***The RCA retains this final paragraph of the original Article 36, choosing to recognize that the confession was written within a historical context which may not accurately describe the situation that pertains today. Synod 1985 of the CRC directed that this paragraph be taken from the body of the text and placed in a footnote.

Article 37: The Last Judgment
Finally we believe,
according to God's Word,
that when the time appointed by the Lord is come
(which is unknown to all creatures)
and the number of the elect is complete,
our Lord Jesus Christ will come from heaven,
    bodily and visibly,
as he ascended,
    with great glory and majesty,
to declare himself the judge
    of the living and the dead.
He will burn this old world,
    in fire and flame,
    in order to cleanse it.

Then all human creatures will appear in person
before the great judge—
    men, women, and children,
    who have lived from the beginning until the end
    of the world.
They will be summoned there
"with the archangel's call
and with the sound of God's trumpet."[81]

For all those who died before that time
will be raised from the earth,
    their spirits being joined and united
    with their own bodies
    in which they lived.

And as for those who are still alive,
they will not die like the others
but will be changed "in the twinkling of an eye"
from perishable to imperishable.[82]

Then the books (that is, the consciences) will be opened,
and the dead will be judged
    according to the things they did in the world,[83]
    whether good or evil.
Indeed, all people will give account
of all the idle words they have spoken,[84]
    which the world regards
    as only playing games.
And then the secrets and hypocrisies of all people
will be publicly uncovered
in the sight of all.

Therefore,
with good reason
the thought of this judgment
is horrible and dreadful
to wicked and evil people.
But it is very pleasant
and a great comfort
to the righteous and elect,
    since their total redemption
    will then be accomplished.
They will then receive the fruits of their labor
    and of the trouble they have suffered;
their innocence will be openly recognized by all;
and they will see the terrible vengeance
    that God will bring on the evil ones
    who tyrannized, oppressed, and tormented them
        in this world.

The evil ones will be convicted
    by the witness of their own consciences,
and shall be made immortal—
    but only to be tormented
    in "the eternal fire
        prepared for the devil and his angels."[85]

In contrast,
the faithful and elect will be crowned
    with glory and honor.

The Son of God will profess their names[86]
   before God his Father and the holy and elect angels;
all tears will be wiped from their eyes;[87]
and their cause—
   at present condemned as heretical and evil
   by many judges and civil officers—
will be acknowledged as the cause of the Son of God.

And as a gracious reward
the Lord will make them possess a glory
such as the human heart
could never imagine.

So we look forward to that great day with longing
in order to enjoy fully
the promises of God in Christ Jesus,
our Lord.

[81] 1 Thess. 4:16
[82] 1 Cor. 15:51-53
[83] Rev. 20:12
[84] Matt. 12:36
[85] Matt. 25:41
[86] Matt. 10:32
[87] Rev. 7:17

The Heidelberg Catechism

Introduction

The Heidelberg Catechism (1563) was composed in the city of Heidelberg, Germany, at the request of Elector Frederick III, who ruled the province of the Palatinate from 1559 to 1576. The new catechism was intended as a tool for teaching young people, a guide for preaching in the provincial churches, and a form of confessional unity among the several Protestant factions in the Palatinate. An old tradition credits Zacharias Ursinus and Caspar Olevianus with being the coauthors of the catechism, but the project was actually the work of a team of ministers and university theologians under the watchful eye of Frederick himself. Ursinus probably served as the primary writer on the team, and Olevianus had a lesser role. The catechism was approved by a synod in Heidelberg in January 1563. A second and third German edition, each with small additions, as well as a Latin translation were published the same year in Heidelberg. The third edition was included in the Palatinate Church Order of November 15, 1563, at which time the catechism was divided into fifty-two sections or Lord's Days, so that one Lord's Day could be explained in an afternoon worship service each Sunday of the year.

The Synod of Dort approved the Heidelberg Catechism in 1619, and it soon became the most ecumenical of the Reformed catechisms and confessions. It has been translated into many European, Asian, and African languages and is still the most widely used and warmly praised catechism of the Reformation period.

Most of the footnoted biblical references in this translation of the catechism were included in the early German and Latin editions, but the precise selection was approved by Synod 1975 of the Christian Reformed Church.

LORD'S DAY 1

1   Q. **What is your only comfort
in life and in death?**

     A.   That I am not my own,[1]
but belong—
     body and soul,
     in life and in death—[2]
to my faithful Savior, Jesus Christ.[3]

       He has fully paid for all my sins with his precious blood,[4]
and has set me free from the tyranny of the devil.[5]
He also watches over me in such a way[6]
that not a hair can fall from my head
without the will of my Father in heaven;[7]
in fact, all things must work together for my salvation.[8]

Because I belong to him,
Christ, by his Holy Spirit,
assures me of eternal life[9]
and makes me wholeheartedly willing and ready
from now on to live for him.[10]

[1] 1 Cor. 6:19-20
[2] Rom. 14:7-9
[3] 1 Cor. 3:23; Titus 2:14
[4] 1 Pet. 1:18-19; 1 John 1:7-9; 2:2
[5] John 8:34-36; Heb. 2:14-15; 1 John 3:1-11
[6] John 6:39-40; 10:27-30; 2 Thess. 3:3; 1 Pet. 1:5
[7] Matt. 10:29-31; Luke 21:16-18
[8] Rom. 8:28
[9] Rom. 8:15-16; 2 Cor. 1:21-22; 5:5; Eph. 1:13-14
[10] Rom. 8:1-17

2   **Q. What must you know to
live and die in the joy of this comfort?**

      A. Three things:

first, how great my sin and misery are;[1]
second, how I am set free from all my sins and misery;[2]
third, how I am to thank God for such deliverance.[3]

[1] Rom. 3:9-10; 1 John 1:10
[2] John 17:3; Acts 4:12; 10:43
[3] Matt. 5:16; Rom. 6:13; Eph. 5:8-10; 2 Tim. 2:15; 1 Pet. 2:9-10

Part I: Misery

LORD'S DAY 2

3   **Q. How do you come to know your misery?**

      A. The law of God tells me.[1]

[1] Rom. 3:20; 7:7-25

4   **Q. What does God's law require of us?**

      A. Christ teaches us this in summary in Matthew 22:37-40:

"'You shall love the Lord your God
with all your heart,
and with all your soul,
and with all your mind.'[1]
This is the greatest and first commandment.

"And a second is like it:
'You shall love your neighbor as yourself.'[2]

"On these two commandments hang
all the law and the prophets."

[1] Deut. 6:5
[2] Lev. 19:18

5   **Q. Can you live up to all this perfectly?**
      A. No.[1]
         I have a natural tendency
         to hate God and my neighbor.[2]

[1] Rom. 3:9-20, 23; 1 John 1:8, 10
[2] Gen. 6:5; Jer. 17:9; Rom. 7:23-24; 8:7; Eph. 2:1-3; Titus 3:3

LORD'S DAY 3

6   **Q. Did God create people
         so wicked and perverse?**
      A. No.
         God created them good[1] and in his own image,[2]
            that is, in true righteousness and holiness,[3]
         so that they might
            truly know God their creator,[4]
            love him with all their heart,
            and live with God in eternal happiness,
         to praise and glorify him.[5]

[1] Gen. 1:31
[2] Gen. 1:26-27
[3] Eph. 4:24
[4] Col. 3:10
[5] Ps. 8

7   **Q. Then where does this corrupt human nature come from?**
      A. The fall and disobedience of our first parents,
            Adam and Eve, in Paradise.[1]
         This fall has so poisoned our nature[2]
            that we are all conceived and born
            in a sinful condition.[3]

[1] Gen. 3
[2] Rom. 5:12, 18-19
[3] Ps. 51:5

8 Q. But are we so corrupt
that we are totally unable to do any good
and inclined toward all evil?

A. Yes,[1] unless we are born again
by the Spirit of God.[2]

[1] Gen. 6:5; 8:21; Job 14:4; Isa. 53:6
[2] John 3:3-5

LORD'S DAY 4

9 Q. But doesn't God do us an injustice
by requiring in his law
what we are unable to do?

A. No, God created human beings with the ability to keep the law.[1]
They, however, provoked by the devil,[2]
in willful disobedience,[3]
robbed themselves and all their descendants of these gifts.[4]

[1] Gen. 1:31; Eph. 4:24
[2] Gen. 3:13; John 8:44
[3] Gen. 3:6
[4] Rom. 5:12, 18, 19

10 Q. Does God permit
such disobedience and rebellion
to go unpunished?

A. Certainly not.
God is terribly angry
with the sin we are born with
as well as the sins we personally commit.

As a just judge,
God will punish them both now and in eternity,[1]
having declared:
"Cursed is everyone who does not observe and obey
all the things written in the book of the law."[2]

[1] Ex. 34:7; Ps. 5:4-6; Nah. 1:2; Rom. 1:18; Eph. 5:6; Heb. 9:27
[2] Gal. 3:10; Deut. 27:26

11 Q. But isn't God also merciful?

A. God is certainly merciful,[1]
but also just.[2]
God's justice demands
that sin, committed against his supreme majesty,
be punished with the supreme penalty—
eternal punishment of body and soul.[3]

[1] Ex. 34:6-7; Ps. 103:8-9
[2] Ex. 34:7; Deut. 7:9-11; Ps. 5:4-6; Heb. 10:30-31
[3] Matt. 25:35-46

Part II: Deliverance

LORD'S DAY 5

**12 Q. According to God's righteous judgment
we deserve punishment
both now and in eternity:
how then can we escape this punishment
and return to God's favor?**

A. God requires that his justice be satisfied.[1]
Therefore the claims of this justice
must be paid in full,
either by ourselves or by another.[2]

[1] Ex. 23:7; Rom. 2:1-11
[2] Isa. 53:11; Rom. 8:3-4

13 Q. Can we make this payment ourselves?

A. Certainly not.
Actually, we increase our debt every day.[1]

[1] Matt. 6:12; Rom. 2:4-5

**14 Q. Can another creature—any at all—
pay this debt for us?**

A. No.
To begin with,
God will not punish any other creature
for what a human is guilty of.[1]
Furthermore,
no mere creature can bear the weight
of God's eternal wrath against sin
and deliver others from it.[2]

[1] Ezek. 18:4, 20; Heb. 2:14-18
[2] Ps. 49:7-9; 130:3

15 Q. **What kind of mediator and deliverer
should we look for then?**

A. One who is a true[1] and righteous[2] human,
yet more powerful than all creatures,
that is, one who is also true God.[3]

[1] Rom. 1:3; 1 Cor. 15:21; Heb. 2:17
[2] Isa. 53:9; 2 Cor. 5:21; Heb. 7:26
[3] Isa. 7:14; 9:6; Jer. 23:6; John 1:1

LORD'S DAY 6

16 Q. **Why must the mediator be a true and righteous human?**

A. God's justice demands
that human nature, which has sinned,
must pay for sin;[1]
but a sinful human could never pay for others.[2]

[1] Rom. 5:12, 15; 1 Cor. 15:21; Heb. 2:14-16
[2] Heb. 7:26-27; 1 Pet. 3:18

17 Q. **Why must the mediator also be true God?**

A. So that the mediator,
by the power of his divinity,
might bear the weight of God's wrath in his humanity
and earn for us
and restore to us
righteousness and life.[1]

[1] Isa. 53; John 3:16; 2 Cor. 5:21

18 Q. **Then who is this mediator—
true God and at the same time
a true and righteous human?**

A. Our Lord Jesus Christ,[1]
who was given to us
to completely deliver us
and make us right with God.[2]

[1] Matt. 1:21-23; Luke 2:11; 1 Tim. 2:5
[2] 1 Cor. 1:30

19 Q. **How do you come to know this?**

A. The holy gospel tells me.
God began to reveal the gospel already in Paradise;[1]
later God proclaimed it
by the holy patriarchs[2] and prophets[3]

and foreshadowed it
> by the sacrifices and other ceremonies of the law;[4]
and finally God fulfilled it
> through his own beloved Son.[5]

[1] Gen. 3:15
[2] Gen. 22:18; 49:10
[3] Isa. 53; Jer. 23:5-6; Mic. 7:18-20; Acts 10:43; Heb. 1:1-2
[4] Lev. 1-7; John 5:46; Heb. 10:1-10
[5] Rom. 10:4; Gal. 4:4-5; Col. 2:17

LORD'S DAY 7

**20 Q. Are all people then saved through Christ
just as they were lost through Adam?**

   A. No.
Only those are saved
who through true faith
> are grafted into Christ
> and accept all his benefits.[1]

[1] Matt. 7:14; John 3:16, 18, 36; Rom. 11:16-21

21 Q. What is true faith?

   A. True faith is
not only a sure knowledge by which I hold as true
> all that God has revealed to us in Scripture;[1]
it is also a wholehearted trust,[2]
> which the Holy Spirit creates in me[3] by the gospel,[4]
> that God has freely granted,
> > not only to others but to me also,[5]
> > > forgiveness of sins,
> > > eternal righteousness,
> > > and salvation.[6]
These are gifts of sheer grace,
granted solely by Christ's merit.[7]

[1] John 17:3, 17; Heb. 11:1-3; James 2:19
[2] Rom. 4:18-21; 5:1; 10:10; Heb. 4:14-16
[3] Matt. 16:15-17; John 3:5; Acts 16:14
[4] Rom. 1:16; 10:17; 1 Cor. 1:21
[5] Gal. 2:20
[6] Rom. 1:17; Heb. 10:10
[7] Rom. 3:21-26; Gal. 2:16; Eph. 2:8-10

22 Q. What then must a Christian believe?

A. All that is promised us in the gospel,[1]
a summary of which is taught us
in the articles of our universal
and undisputed Christian faith.

[1] Matt. 28:18-20; John 20:30-31

23 Q. What are these articles?

A. I believe in God, the Father almighty,
creator of heaven and earth.

I believe in Jesus Christ, his only begotten Son, our Lord,
who was conceived by the Holy Spirit
and born of the virgin Mary.
He suffered under Pontius Pilate,
was crucified, died, and was buried;
he descended to hell.
The third day he rose again from the dead.
He ascended to heaven
and is seated at the right hand of God the Father almighty.
From there he will come to judge the living and the dead.

I believe in the Holy Spirit,
the holy catholic church,
the communion of saints,
the forgiveness of sins,
the resurrection of the body,
and the life everlasting. Amen.

LORD'S DAY 8

24 Q. How are these articles divided?

A. Into three parts:
God the Father and our creation;
God the Son and our deliverance;
and God the Holy Spirit and our sanctification.

**25 Q. Since there is only one divine being,[1]
why do you speak of three:
Father, Son, and Holy Spirit?**

A. Because that is how
God has revealed himself in his Word:[2]
these three distinct persons
are one, true, eternal God.

[1] Deut. 6:4; 1 Cor. 8:4, 6
[2] Matt. 3:16-17; 28:18-19; Luke 4:18 (Isa. 61:1); John 14:26; 15:26; 2 Cor. 13:14; Gal. 4:6; Tit. 3:5-6

LORD'S DAY 9

26 Q. **What do you believe when you say,**
   "I believe in God, the Father almighty,
   creator of heaven and earth"?

A. That the eternal Father of our Lord Jesus Christ,
      who out of nothing created heaven and earth
         and everything in them,[1]
      who still upholds and rules them
         by his eternal counsel and providence,[2]
   is my God and Father
      because of Christ the Son.[3]

   I trust God so much that I do not doubt
      he will provide
         whatever I need
         for body and soul,[4]
      and will turn to my good
         whatever adversity he sends upon me
         in this sad world.[5]

   God is able to do this because he is almighty God[6]
   and desires to do this because he is a faithful Father.[7]

[1] Gen. 1-2; Ex. 20:11; Ps. 33:6; Isa. 44:24; Acts 4:24; 14:15
[2] Ps. 104; Matt. 6:30; 10:29; Eph. 1:11
[3] John 1:12-13; Rom. 8:15-16; Gal. 4:4-7; Eph. 1:5
[4] Ps. 55:22; Matt. 6:25-26; Luke 12:22-31
[5] Rom. 8:28
[6] Gen. 18:14; Rom. 8:31-39
[7] Matt. 7:9-11

LORD'S DAY 10

27 Q. **What do you understand**
   by the providence of God?

A. The almighty and ever present power of God[1]
      by which God upholds, as with his hand,
         heaven
         and earth
         and all creatures,[2]
      and so rules them that
         leaf and blade,
         rain and drought,
         fruitful and lean years,
         food and drink,
         health and sickness,

          prosperity and poverty—[3]
          all things, in fact,
          come to us
              not by chance[4]
              but by his fatherly hand.[5]

[1] Jer. 23:23-24; Acts 17:24-28
[2] Heb. 1:3
[3] Jer. 5:24; Acts 14:15-17; John 9:3; Prov. 22:2
[4] Prov. 16:33
[5] Matt. 10:29

**28 Q. How does the knowledge
        of God's creation and providence help us?**
     A. We can be patient when things go against us,[1]
          thankful when things go well,[2]
          and for the future we can have
          good confidence in our faithful God and Father
          that nothing in creation will separate us from his love.[3]
          For all creatures are so completely in God's hand
              that without his will
              they can neither move nor be moved.[4]

[1] Job 1:21-22; James 1:3
[2] Deut. 8:10; 1 Thess. 5:18
[3] Ps. 55:22; Rom. 5:3-5; 8:38-39
[4] Job 1:12; 2:6; Prov. 21:1; Acts 17:24-28

God the Son

LORD'S DAY 11

**29 Q. Why is the Son of God called "Jesus,"
        meaning "savior"?**
     A. Because he saves us from our sins,[1]
          and because salvation should not be sought
          and cannot be found in anyone else.[2]

[1] Matt. 1:21; Heb. 7:25
[2] Isa. 43:11; John 15:5; Acts 4:11-12; 1 Tim. 2:5

**30 Q. Do those who look for
their salvation in saints,
in themselves, or elsewhere
really believe in the only savior Jesus?**

A. No.
Although they boast of being his,
by their actions they deny
the only savior, Jesus.[1]

Either Jesus is not a perfect savior,
or those who in true faith accept this savior
have in him all they need for their salvation.[2]

[1] 1 Cor. 1:12-13; Gal. 5:4
[2] Col. 1:19-20; 2:10; 1 John 1:7

LORD'S DAY 12

**31 Q. Why is he called "Christ,"
meaning "anointed"?**

A. Because he has been ordained by God the Father
and has been anointed with the Holy Spirit[1]
to be
our chief prophet and teacher[2]
who fully reveals to us
the secret counsel and will of God concerning our deliverance;[3]
our only high priest[4]
who has delivered us by the one sacrifice of his body,[5]
and who continually pleads our cause with the Father;[6]
and our eternal king[7]
who governs us by his Word and Spirit,
and who guards us and keeps us
in the freedom he has won for us.[8]

[1] Luke 3:21-22; 4:14-19 (Isa. 61:1); Heb. 1:9 (Ps. 45:7)
[2] Acts 3:22 (Deut. 18:15)
[3] John 1:18; 15:15
[4] Heb. 7:17 (Ps. 110:4)
[5] Heb. 9:12; 10:11-14
[6] Rom. 8:34; Heb. 9:24
[7] Matt. 21:5 (Zech. 9:9)
[8] Matt. 28:18-20; John 10:28; Rev. 12:10-11

32 Q. But why are you called a Christian?
    A. Because by faith I am a member of Christ[1]
       and so I share in his anointing.[2]
          I am anointed
          to confess his name,[3]
          to present myself to him as a living sacrifice of thanks,[4]
          to strive with a free conscience against sin and the devil
             in this life,[5]
          and afterward to reign with Christ
             over all creation
             for eternity.[6]

[1] 1 Cor. 12:12-27
[2] Acts 2:17 (Joel 2:28); 1 John 2:27
[3] Matt. 10:32; Rom. 10:9-10; Heb. 13:15
[4] Rom. 12:1; 1 Pet. 2:5, 9
[5] Gal. 5:16-17; Eph. 6:11; 1 Tim. 1:18-19
[6] Matt. 25:34; 2 Tim. 2:12

LORD'S DAY 13

**33 Q. Why is he called God's "only begotten Son"
      when we also are God's children?**
    A. Because Christ alone is the eternal, natural Son of God.[1]
      We, however, are adopted children of God—
         adopted by grace through Christ.[2]

[1] John 1:1-3, 14, 18; Heb. 1
[2] John 1:12; Rom. 8:14-17; Eph. 1:5-6

34 Q. Why do you call him "our Lord"?
    A. Because—
          not with gold or silver,
          but with his precious blood—[1]
      he has set us free
          from sin and from the tyranny of the devil,[2]
      and has bought us,
          body and soul,
      to be his very own.[3]

[1] 1 Pet. 1:18-19
[2] Col. 1:13-14; Heb. 2:14-15
[3] 1 Cor. 6:20; 1 Tim. 2:5-6

35 Q. **What does it mean that he
"was conceived by the Holy Spirit
and born of the virgin Mary"?**

A. That the eternal Son of God,
who is and remains
true and eternal God,[1]
took to himself,
through the working of the Holy Spirit,[2]
from the flesh and blood of the virgin Mary,[3]
a truly human nature
so that he might also become David's true descendant,[4]
like his brothers and sisters in every way[5]
except for sin.[6]

[1] John 1:1; 10:30-36; Acts 13:33 (Ps. 2:7); Col. 1:15-17; 1 John 5:20
[2] Luke 1:35
[3] Matt. 1:18-23; John 1:14; Gal. 4:4; Heb. 2:14
[4] 2 Sam. 7:12-16; Ps. 132:11; Matt. 1:1; Rom. 1:3
[5] Phil. 2:7; Heb. 2:17
[6] Heb. 4:15; 7:26-27

36 Q. **How does the holy conception and birth of Christ
benefit you?**

A. He is our mediator[1]
and, in God's sight,
he covers with his innocence and perfect holiness
my sinfulness in which I was conceived.[2]

[1] 1 Tim. 2:5-6; Heb. 9:13-15
[2] Rom. 8:3-4; 2 Cor. 5:21; Gal. 4:4-5; 1 Pet. 1:18-19

LORD'S DAY 15

37 Q. **What do you understand
by the word "suffered"?**

A. That during his whole life on earth,
but especially at the end,
Christ sustained
in body and soul
the wrath of God against the sin of the whole human race.[1]

This he did in order that,
    by his suffering as the only atoning sacrifice,[2]
    he might deliver us, body and soul,
        from eternal condemnation,[3]
    and gain for us
        God's grace,
        righteousness,
        and eternal life.[4]

[1] Isa. 53; 1 Pet. 2:24; 3:18
[2] Rom. 3:25; Heb. 10:14; 1 John 2:2; 4:10
[3] Rom. 8:1-4; Gal. 3:13
[4] John 3:16; Rom. 3:24-26

**38 Q. Why did he suffer
"under Pontius Pilate" as judge?**

    A. So that he,
        though innocent,
    might be condemned by an earthly judge,[1]
    and so free us from the severe judgment of God
        that was to fall on us.[2]

[1] Luke 23:13-24; John 19:4, 12-16
[2] Isa. 53:4-5; 2 Cor. 5:21; Gal. 3:13

**39 Q. Is it significant that he was "crucified"
instead of dying some other way?**

    A. Yes.
    By this I am convinced
    that he shouldered the curse
    which lay on me,
    since death by crucifixion was cursed by God.[1]

[1] Gal. 3:10-13 (Deut. 21:23)

40 Q. Why did Christ have to suffer death?

A. Because God's justice and truth require it: [1]
   nothing else could pay for our sins
   except the death of the Son of God.[2]

[1] Gen. 2:17
[2] Rom. 8:3-4; Phil. 2:8; Heb. 2:9

41 Q. Why was he "buried"?

A. His burial testifies
   that he really died.[1]

[1] Isa. 53:9; John 19:38-42; Acts 13:29; 1 Cor. 15:3-4

**42 Q. Since Christ has died for us,
       why do we still have to die?**

A. Our death does not pay the debt of our sins.[1]
   Rather, it puts an end to our sinning
   and is our entrance into eternal life.[2]

[1] Ps. 49:7
[2] John 5:24; Phil. 1:21-23; 1 Thess. 5:9-10

**43 Q. What further benefit do we receive
       from Christ's sacrifice and death on the cross?**

A. By Christ's power
   our old selves are crucified, put to death, and buried with him,[1]
   so that the evil desires of the flesh
       may no longer rule us,[2]
   but that instead we may offer ourselves
       as a sacrifice of gratitude to him.[3]

[1] Rom. 6:5-11; Col. 2:11-12
[2] Rom. 6:12-14
[3] Rom. 12:1; Eph. 5:1-2

**44 Q. Why does the creed add,
       "He descended to hell"?**

A. To assure me during attacks of deepest dread and temptation
   that Christ my Lord,
       by suffering unspeakable anguish, pain, and terror of soul,
           on the cross but also earlier,
       has delivered me from hellish anguish and torment.[1]

[1] Isa. 53; Matt. 26:36-46; 27:45-46; Luke 22:44; Heb. 5:7-10

**45 Q. How does Christ's resurrection
benefit us?**

A. First, by his resurrection he has overcome death,
so that he might make us share in the righteousness
he obtained for us by his death.[1]

Second, by his power we too
are already raised to a new life.[2]

Third, Christ's resurrection
is a sure pledge to us of our blessed resurrection.[3]

[1] Rom. 4:25; 1 Cor. 15:16-20; 1 Pet. 1:3-5
[2] Rom. 6:5-11; Eph. 2:4-6; Col. 3:1-4
[3] Rom. 8:11; 1 Cor. 15:12-23; Phil. 3:20-21

LORD'S DAY 18

**46 Q. What do you mean by saying,
"He ascended to heaven"?**

A. That Christ,
while his disciples watched,
was taken up from the earth into heaven[1]
and remains there on our behalf[2]
until he comes again
to judge the living and the dead.[3]

[1] Luke 24:50-51; Acts 1:9-11
[2] Rom. 8:34; Eph. 4:8-10; Heb. 7:23-25; 9:24
[3] Acts 1:11

**47 Q. But isn't Christ with us
until the end of the world
as he promised us?[1]**

A. Christ is true human and true God.
In his human nature Christ is not now on earth;[2]
but in his divinity, majesty, grace, and Spirit
he is never absent from us.[3]

[1] Matt. 28:20
[2] Acts 1:9-11; 3:19-21
[3] Matt. 28:18-20; John 14:16-19

**48 Q. If his humanity is not present
wherever his divinity is,
then aren't the two natures of Christ
separated from each other?**

A. Certainly not.
Since divinity
is not limited
and is present everywhere,[1]
it is evident that
Christ's divinity is surely beyond the bounds of
the humanity that has been taken on,
but at the same time his divinity is in
and remains personally united to
his humanity.[2]

[1] Jer. 23:23-24; Acts 7:48-49 (Isa. 66:1)
[2] John 1:14; 3:13; Col. 2:9

**49 Q. How does Christ's ascension to heaven
benefit us?**

A. First, he is our advocate
in heaven
in the presence of his Father.[1]

Second, we have our own flesh in heaven
as a sure pledge that Christ our head
will also take us, his members,
up to himself.[2]

Third, he sends his Spirit to us on earth
as a corresponding pledge.[3]
By the Spirit's power
we seek not earthly things
but the things above, where Christ is,
sitting at God's right hand.[4]

[1] Rom. 8:34; 1 John 2:1
[2] John 14:2; 17:24; Eph. 2:4-6
[3] John 14:16; 2 Cor. 1:21-22; 5:5
[4] Col. 3:1-4

50　Q.　**Why the next words:**
　　　　"and is seated at the right hand of God"?

　　A.　Because Christ ascended to heaven
　　　　　to show there that he is head of his church,[1]
　　　　　　　the one through whom the Father rules all things.[2]

[1] Eph. 1:20-23; Col. 1:18
[2] Matt. 28:18; John 5:22-23

51　Q.　**How does this glory of Christ our head**
　　　　benefit us?

　　A.　First, through his Holy Spirit
　　　　　he pours out gifts from heaven
　　　　　　upon us his members.[1]

　　　　Second, by his power
　　　　　he defends us and keeps us safe
　　　　　　from all enemies.[2]

[1] Acts 2:33; Eph. 4:7-12
[2] Ps. 110:1-2; John 10:27-30; Rev. 19:11-16

52　Q.　**How does Christ's return**
　　　　"to judge the living and the dead"
　　　　comfort you?

　　A.　In all distress and persecution,
　　　　　with uplifted head,
　　　　　I confidently await the very judge
　　　　　　who has already offered himself to the judgment of God
　　　　　　in my place and removed the whole curse from me.[1]
　　　　Christ will cast all his enemies and mine
　　　　　into everlasting condemnation,
　　　　but will take me and all his chosen ones
　　　　　to himself
　　　　　into the joy and glory of heaven.[2]

[1] Luke 21:28; Rom. 8:22-25; Phil. 3:20-21; Tit. 2:13-14
[2] Matt. 25:31-46; 2 Thess. 1:6-10

LORD'S DAY 20

53 **Q.** **What do you believe
concerning "the Holy Spirit"?**

A. First, that the Spirit, with the Father and the Son,
is eternal God.[1]

Second, that the Spirit is given also to me,[2]
so that, through true faith,
he makes me share in Christ and all his benefits,[3]
comforts me,[4]
and will remain with me forever.[5]

[1] Gen. 1:1-2; Matt. 28:19; Acts 5:3-4
[2] 1 Cor. 6:19; 2 Cor. 1:21-22; Gal. 4:6
[3] Gal. 3:14
[4] John 15:26; Acts 9:31
[5] John 14:16-17; 1 Pet. 4:14

LORD'S DAY 21

54 **Q.** **What do you believe
concerning "the holy catholic church"?**

A. I believe that the Son of God
through his Spirit and Word,[1]
out of the entire human race,[2]
from the beginning of the world to its end,[3]
gathers, protects, and preserves for himself
a community chosen for eternal life[4]
and united in true faith.[5]
And of this community I am[6] and always will be[7]
a living member.

[1] John 10:14-16; Acts 20:28; Rom. 10:14-17; Col. 1:18
[2] Gen. 26:3b-4; Rev. 5:9
[3] Isa. 59:21; 1 Cor. 11:26
[4] Matt. 16:18; John 10:28-30; Rom. 8:28-30; Eph. 1:3-14
[5] Acts 2:42-47; Eph. 4:1-6
[6] 1 John 3:14, 19-21
[7] John 10:27-28; 1 Cor. 1:4-9; 1 Pet. 1:3-5

55 **Q.** **What do you understand by
"the communion of saints"?**

A. First, that believers one and all,
as members of this community,
share in Christ
and in all his treasures and gifts.[1]

Second, that each member
should consider it a duty
to use these gifts
readily and joyfully
for the service and enrichment
of the other members.[2]

[1] Rom. 8:32; 1 Cor. 6:17; 12:4-7, 12-13; 1 John 1:3
[2] Rom. 12:4-8; 1 Cor. 12:20-27; 13:1-7; Phil. 2:4-8

56 Q. **What do you believe**
    concerning "the forgiveness of sins"?
    A. I believe that God,
            because of Christ's satisfaction,
        will no longer remember
            any of my sins[1]
        or my sinful nature
                which I need to struggle against all my life.[2]

        Rather, by grace
            God grants me the righteousness of Christ
            to free me forever from judgment.[3]

[1] Ps. 103:3-4, 10, 12; Mic. 7:18-19; 2 Cor. 5:18-21; 1 John 1:7; 2:2
[2] Rom. 7:21-25
[3] John 3:17-18; Rom. 8:1-2

LORD'S DAY 22

57 Q. **How does "the resurrection of the body"**
    comfort you?
    A. Not only will my soul
            be taken immediately after this life
            to Christ its head,[1]
        but also my very flesh will be
            raised by the power of Christ,
            reunited with my soul,
            and made like Christ's glorious body.[2]

[1] Luke 23:43; Phil. 1:21-23
[2] 1 Cor. 15:20, 42-46, 54; Phil. 3:21; 1 John 3:2

58 Q. How does the article concerning "life everlasting" comfort you?

A. Even as I already now
    experience in my heart
    the beginning of eternal joy,[1]
so after this life I will have
    perfect blessedness such as
        no eye has seen,
        no ear has heard,
        no human heart has ever imagined:
a blessedness in which to praise God forever.[2]

[1] Rom. 14:17
[2] John 17:3; 1 Cor. 2:9

LORD'S DAY 23

59 Q. What good does it do you, however, to believe all this?

A. In Christ I am righteous before God
and heir to life everlasting.[1]

[1] John 3:36; Rom. 1:17 (Hab. 2:4); Rom. 5:1-2

60 Q. How are you righteous before God?

A. Only by true faith in Jesus Christ.[1]

Even though my conscience accuses me
    of having grievously sinned against all God's commandments,
    of never having kept any of them,[2]
    and of still being inclined toward all evil,[3]
nevertheless,
    without any merit of my own,[4]
    out of sheer grace,[5]
God grants and credits to me
the perfect satisfaction, righteousness, and holiness of Christ,[6]
    as if I had never sinned nor been a sinner,
    and as if I had been as perfectly obedient
        as Christ was obedient for me.[7]

All I need to do
is accept this gift with a believing heart.[8]

[1] Rom. 3:21-28; Gal. 2:16; Eph. 2:8-9; Phil 3:8-11
[2] Rom. 3:9-10
[3] Rom. 7:23
[4] Tit. 3:4-5
[5] Rom. 3:24; Eph. 2:8
[6] Rom. 4:3-5 (Gen. 15:6); 2 Cor. 5:17-19; 1 John 2:1-2
[7] Rom. 4:24-25; 2 Cor. 5:21
[8] John 3:18; Acts 16:30-31

**61 Q. Why do you say that
through faith alone
you are righteous?**

A. Not because I please God
by the worthiness of my faith.
It is because only Christ's satisfaction, righteousness, and holiness
make me righteous before God,[1]
and because I can accept this righteousness and make it mine
in no other way
than through faith.[2]

[1] 1 Cor. 1:30-31
[2] Rom. 10:10; 1 John 5:10-12

LORD'S DAY 24

**62 Q. Why can't our good works
be our righteousness before God,
or at least a part of our righteousness?**

A. Because the righteousness
which can pass God's judgment
must be entirely perfect
and must in every way measure up to the divine law.[1]
But even our best works in this life
are imperfect
and stained with sin.[2]

[1] Rom. 3:20; Gal. 3:10 (Deut. 27:26)
[2] Isa. 64:6

63 Q. **How can our good works**
    be said to merit nothing
    when God promises to reward them
    in this life and the next?[1]
    A. This reward is not earned;
        it is a gift of grace.[2]

[1] Matt. 5:12; Heb. 11:6
[2] Luke 17:10; 2 Tim. 4:7-8

64 Q. **But doesn't this teaching**
    make people indifferent and wicked?
    A. No.
        It is impossible
            for those grafted into Christ through true faith
        not to produce fruits of gratitude.[1]

[1] Luke 6:43-45; John 15:5

The Holy Sacraments

LORD'S DAY 25

65 Q. **It is through faith alone**
    that we share in Christ and all his benefits:
    where then does that faith come from?
    A. The Holy Spirit produces it in our hearts[1]
            by the preaching of the holy gospel,[2]
        and confirms it
            by the use of the holy sacraments.[3]

[1] John 3:5; 1 Cor. 2:10-14; Eph. 2:8
[2] Rom. 10:17; 1 Pet. 1:23-25
[3] Matt. 28:19-20; 1 Cor. 10:16

66 Q. **What are sacraments?**
    A. Sacraments are visible, holy signs and seals.
        They were instituted by God so that
            by our use of them
        he might make us understand more clearly
            the promise of the gospel,
        and seal that promise.[1]

And this is God's gospel promise:
    to grant us forgiveness of sins and eternal life
      by grace
      because of Christ's one sacrifice
      accomplished on the cross.[2]

[1] Gen. 17:11; Deut. 30:6; Rom. 4:11
[2] Matt. 26:27-28; Acts 2:38; Heb. 10:10

67 **Q.** **Are both the word and the sacraments then**
      intended to focus our faith
      on the sacrifice of Jesus Christ on the cross
      as the only ground of our salvation?
    A. Yes!
      In the gospel the Holy Spirit teaches us
      and by the holy sacraments confirms
        that our entire salvation
        rests on Christ's one sacrifice for us on the cross.[1]

[1] Rom. 6:3; 1 Cor. 11:26; Gal. 3:27

68 **Q.** **How many sacraments**
      did Christ institute in the New Testament?
    A. Two: holy baptism and the holy supper.[1]

[1] Matt. 28:19-20; 1 Cor. 11:23-26

Holy Baptism

LORD'S DAY 26

69 **Q.** **How does holy baptism**
      remind and assure you
      that Christ's one sacrifice on the cross
      benefits you personally?
    A. In this way:
      Christ instituted this outward washing[1]
      and with it promised that,
        as surely as water washes away the dirt from the body,
        so certainly his blood and his Spirit
        wash away my soul's impurity,
          that is, all my sins.[2]

[1] Acts 2:38
[2] Matt. 3:11; Rom. 6:3-10; 1 Pet. 3:21

70 Q. **What does it mean
to be washed with Christ's blood and Spirit?**

A. To be washed with Christ's blood means
that God, by grace, has forgiven our sins
because of Christ's blood
poured out for us in his sacrifice on the cross.[1]

To be washed with Christ's Spirit means
that the Holy Spirit has renewed
and sanctified us to be members of Christ,
so that more and more
we become dead to sin
and live holy and blameless lives.[2]

[1] Zech. 13:1; Eph. 1:7-8; Heb. 12:24; 1 Pet. 1:2; Rev. 1:5
[2] Ezek. 36:25-27; John 3:5-8; Rom. 6:4; 1 Cor. 6:11; Col. 2:11-12

71 Q. **Where does Christ promise
that we are washed with his blood and Spirit
as surely as we are washed
with the water of baptism?**

A. In the institution of baptism, where he says:

"Go therefore and make disciples of all nations,
baptizing them in the name of the Father
and of the Son
and of the Holy Spirit."[1]

"The one who believes and is baptized will be saved;
but the one who does not believe will be condemned."[2]

This promise is repeated when Scripture calls baptism
"the water of rebirth"[3] and
the washing away of sins.[4]

[1] Matt. 28:19
[2] Mark 16:16
[3] Tit. 3:5
[4] Acts 22:16

LORD'S DAY 27

72 Q. **Does this outward washing with water
itself wash away sins?**

A. No, only Jesus Christ's blood and the Holy Spirit
cleanse us from all sins.[1]

[1] Matt. 3:11; 1 Pet. 3:21; 1 John 1:7

**73 Q. Why then does the Holy Spirit call baptism
the water of rebirth and
the washing away of sins?**

A. God has good reason for these words.
To begin with, God wants to teach us that
the blood and Spirit of Christ take away our sins
just as water removes dirt from the body.[1]

But more important,
God wants to assure us, by this divine pledge and sign,
that we are as truly washed of our sins spiritually
as our bodies are washed with water physically.[2]

[1] 1 Cor. 6:11; Rev. 1:5; 7:14
[2] Acts 2:38; Rom. 6:3-4; Gal. 3:27

74 Q. Should infants also be baptized?

A. Yes.
Infants as well as adults
are included in God's covenant and people,[1]
and they, no less than adults, are promised
deliverance from sin through Christ's blood
and the Holy Spirit who produces faith.[2]

Therefore, by baptism, the sign of the covenant,
they too should be incorporated into the Christian church
and distinguished from the children
of unbelievers.[3]
This was done in the Old Testament by circumcision,[4]
which was replaced in the New Testament by baptism.[5]

[1] Gen. 17:7; Matt. 19:14
[2] Isa. 44:1-3; Acts 2:38-39; 16:31
[3] Acts 10:47; 1 Cor. 7:14
[4] Gen. 17:9-14
[5] Col. 2:11-13

LORD'S DAY 28

75 Q. **How does the holy supper**
       remind and assure you
       that you share in
       Christ's one sacrifice on the cross
       and in all his benefits?
    A. In this way:
       Christ has commanded me and all believers
       to eat this broken bread and to drink this cup
       in remembrance of him.
       With this command come these promises:[1]

       First,
           as surely as I see with my eyes
               the bread of the Lord broken for me
               and the cup shared with me,
           so surely
               his body was offered and broken for me
               and his blood poured out for me
                   on the cross.

       Second,
           as surely as
               I receive from the hand of the one who serves,
               and taste with my mouth
                   the bread and cup of the Lord,
                   given me as sure signs of Christ's body and blood,
           so surely
               he nourishes and refreshes my soul for eternal life
               with his crucified body and poured-out blood.

[1] Matt. 26:26-28; Mark 14:22-24; Luke 22:19-20; 1 Cor. 11:23-25

76 Q. **What does it mean**
       to eat the crucified body of Christ
       and to drink his poured-out blood?
    A. It means
           to accept with a believing heart
               the entire suffering and death of Christ
           and thereby
               to receive forgiveness of sins and eternal life.[1]

But it means more.

Through the Holy Spirit, who lives both in Christ and in us,
we are united more and more to Christ's blessed body.[2]
And so, although he is in heaven[3] and we are on earth,
we are flesh of his flesh and bone of his bone.[4]
And we forever live on and are governed by one Spirit,
as the members of our body are by one soul.[5]

[1] John 6:35, 40, 50-54
[2] John 6:55-56; 1 Cor. 12:13
[3] Acts 1:9-11; 1 Cor. 11:26; Col. 3:1
[4] 1 Cor. 6:15-17; Eph. 5:29-30; 1 John 4:13
[5] John 6:56-58; 15:1-6; Eph. 4:15-16; 1 John 3:24

77   Q. Where does Christ promise
to nourish and refresh believers
with his body and blood
as surely as
they eat this broken bread
and drink this cup?

   A. In the institution of the Lord's Supper:

"The Lord Jesus on the night when he was betrayed
took a loaf of bread, and when he had given thanks,
he broke it and said,
    'This is my body that is [broken]* for you.
    Do this in remembrance of me.'
In the same way he took the cup also, after supper, saying,
    'This cup is the new covenant in my blood.
    Do this, as often as you drink it,
    in remembrance of me.'
For as often as you eat this bread and drink the cup,
you proclaim the Lord's death
until he comes."[1]

This promise is repeated by Paul in these words:

"The cup of blessing that we bless,
    is it not a sharing in the blood of Christ?
The bread that we break,
    is it not a sharing in the body of Christ?
Because there is one bread, we who are many are one body,
for we all partake of the one bread."[2]

[1] 1 Cor. 11:23-26
[2] 1 Cor. 10:16-17
*The word "broken" does not appear in the NRSV text, but it was present in the original German of the Heidelberg Catechism.

**78 Q. Do the bread and wine become
the real body and blood of Christ?**

A. No.
Just as the water of baptism
is not changed into Christ's blood
and does not itself wash away sins
but is simply a divine sign and assurance[1] of these things,
so too the holy bread of the Lord's Supper
does not become the actual body of Christ,[2]
even though it is called the body of Christ[3]
in keeping with the nature and language of sacraments.[4]

[1] Eph. 5:26; Tit. 3:5
[2] Matt. 26:26-29
[3] 1 Cor. 10:16-17; 11:26-28
[4] Gen. 17:10-11; Ex. 12:11, 13; 1 Cor. 10:1-4

**79 Q. Why then does Christ call
the bread his body
and the cup his blood,
or the new covenant in his blood,
and Paul use the words,
a sharing in Christ's body and blood?**

A. Christ has good reason for these words.
He wants to teach us that
just as bread and wine nourish the temporal life,
so too his crucified body and poured-out blood
are the true food and drink of our souls for eternal life.[1]

But more important,
he wants to assure us, by this visible sign and pledge,
that we, through the Holy Spirit's work,
share in his true body and blood
as surely as our mouths
receive these holy signs in his remembrance,[2]
and that all of his suffering and obedience
are as definitely ours
as if we personally
had suffered and made satisfaction for our sins.[3]

[1] John 6:51, 55
[2] 1 Cor. 10:16-17; 11:26
[3] Rom. 6:5-11

80* Q. How does the Lord's Supper
   differ from the Roman Catholic Mass?

   A. The Lord's Supper declares to us
      that all our sins are completely forgiven
      through the one sacrifice of Jesus Christ,
      which he himself accomplished on the cross once for all.[1]
   It also declares to us
      that the Holy Spirit grafts us into Christ,[2]
      who with his true body
      is now in heaven at the right hand of the Father[3]
      where he wants us to worship him.[4]

   [But the Mass teaches
      that the living and the dead
      do not have their sins forgiven
      through the suffering of Christ
      unless Christ is still offered for them daily by the priests.
   It also teaches
      that Christ is bodily present
      under the form of bread and wine
      where Christ is therefore to be worshiped.
   Thus the Mass is basically
      nothing but a denial
      of the one sacrifice and suffering of Jesus Christ
      and a condemnable idolatry.]**

[1] John 19:30; Heb. 7:27; 9:12, 25-26; 10:10-18
[2] 1 Cor. 6:17; 10:16-17
[3] Acts 7:55-56; Heb. 1:3; 8:1
[4] Matt. 6:20-21; John 4:21-24; Phil. 3:20; Col. 3:1-3

*Q&A 80 was altogether absent from the first edition of the catechism but was present in a shorter form in the second edition. The translation here given is of the expanded text of the third edition.
**In response to a mandate from Synod 1998, the Christian Reformed Church's Interchurch Relations Committee conducted a study of Q&A 80 and the Roman Catholic Mass. Based on this study, Synod 2004 declared that "Q&A 80 can no longer be held in its current form as part of our confession." Synod 2006 directed that Q&A 80 remain in the CRC's text of the Heidelberg Catechism but that the last three paragraphs be placed in brackets to indicate that they do not accurately reflect the official teaching and practice of today's Roman Catholic Church and are no longer confessionally binding on members of the CRC.

The Reformed Church in America retains the original full text, choosing to recognize that the catechism was written within a historical context which may not accurately describe the Roman Catholic Church's current stance.

81 Q. **Who should come
to the Lord's table?**
A. Those who are displeased with themselves
because of their sins,
but who nevertheless trust
that their sins are pardoned
and that their remaining weakness is covered
by the suffering and death of Christ,
and who also desire more and more
to strengthen their faith
and to lead a better life.

Hypocrites and those who are unrepentant, however,
eat and drink judgment on themselves.[1]

[1] 1 Cor. 10:19-22; 11:26-32

82 Q. **Should those be admitted
to the Lord's Supper
who show by what they profess and how they live
that they are unbelieving and ungodly?**
A. No, that would dishonor God's covenant
and bring down God's wrath upon the entire congregation.[1]
Therefore, according to the instruction of Christ
and his apostles,
the Christian church is duty-bound to exclude such people,
by the official use of the keys of the kingdom,
until they reform their lives.

[1] 1 Cor. 11:17-32; Ps. 50:14-16; Isa. 1:11-17

LORD'S DAY 31

83 Q. **What are the keys of the kingdom?**
A. The preaching of the holy gospel
and Christian discipline toward repentance.
Both of them
open the kingdom of heaven to believers
and close it to unbelievers.[1]

[1] Matt. 16:19; John 20:22-23

84 Q. **How does preaching the holy gospel**
       open and close the kingdom of heaven?
   A. According to the command of Christ:

   The kingdom of heaven is opened
   by proclaiming and publicly declaring
       to all believers, each and every one, that,
       as often as they accept the gospel promise in true faith,
       God, because of Christ's merit,
       truly forgives all their sins.

   The kingdom of heaven is closed, however,
   by proclaiming and publicly declaring
       to unbelievers and hypocrites that,
       as long as they do not repent,
       the wrath of God and eternal condemnation
       rest on them.   .

   God's judgment, both in this life and in the life to come,
   is based on this gospel testimony.[1]

[1] Matt. 16:19; John 3:31-36; 20:21-23

85 Q. **How is the kingdom of heaven**
       closed and opened by Christian discipline?
   A. According to the command of Christ:

   Those who, though called Christians,
       profess unchristian teachings or live unchristian lives,
   and who after repeated personal and loving admonitions,
       refuse to abandon their errors and evil ways,
   and who after being reported to the church, that is,
           to those ordained by the church for that purpose,
       fail to respond also to the church's admonitions—
   such persons the church excludes
           from the Christian community
       by withholding the sacraments from them,
   and God also excludes them from the kingdom of Christ.[1]

   Such persons,
       when promising and demonstrating genuine reform,
   are received again
       as members of Christ
       and of his church.[2]

[1] Matt. 18:15-20; 1 Cor. 5:3-5, 11-13; 2 Thess. 3:14-15
[2] Luke 15:20-24; 2 Cor. 2:6-11

Part III: Gratitude

LORD'S DAY 32

86 Q. **Since we have been delivered
        from our misery
        by grace through Christ
        without any merit of our own,
        why then should we do good works?**
    A. Because Christ, having redeemed us by his blood,
        is also restoring us by his Spirit into his image,
            so that with our whole lives
                we may show that we are thankful to God
                    for his benefits,[1]
            so that he may be praised through us,[2]
            so that we may be assured of our faith by its fruits,[3]
            and so that by our godly living
                our neighbors may be won over to Christ.[4]

[1] Rom. 6:13; 12:1-2; 1 Pet. 2:5-10
[2] Matt. 5:16; 1 Cor. 6:19-20
[3] Matt. 7:17-18; Gal. 5:22-24; 2 Pet. 1:10-11
[4] Matt. 5:14-16; Rom. 14:17-19; 1 Pet. 2:12; 3:1-2

87 Q. **Can those be saved
        who do not turn to God
        from their ungrateful
        and unrepentant ways?**
    A. By no means.
        Scripture tells us that
            no unchaste person,
            no idolater, adulterer, thief,
            no covetous person,
            no drunkard, slanderer, robber,
            or the like
            will inherit the kingdom of God.[1]

[1] 1 Cor. 6:9-10; Gal. 5:19-21; Eph. 5:1-20; 1 John 3:14

LORD'S DAY 33

88 Q. **What is involved
        in genuine repentance or conversion?**
    A. Two things:
            the dying-away of the old self,
            and the rising-to-life of the new.[1]

[1] Rom. 6:1-11; 2 Cor. 5:17; Eph. 4:22-24; Col. 3:5-10

89 Q. What is the dying-away of the old self?
A. To be genuinely sorry for sin
and more and more to hate
and run away from it.[1]

[1] Ps. 51:3-4, 17; Joel 2:12-13; Rom. 8:12-13; 2 Cor. 7:10

90 Q. What is the rising-to-life of the new self?
A. Wholehearted joy in God through Christ[1]
and a love and delight to live
according to the will of God
by doing every kind of good work.[2]

[1] Ps. 51:8, 12; Isa.57:15; Rom. 5:1; 14:17
[2] Rom. 6:10-11; Gal. 2:20

91 Q. What are good works?
A. Only those which
are done out of true faith,[1]
conform to God's law,[2]
and are done for God's glory;[3]
and not those based
on our own opinion
or human tradition.[4]

[1] John 15:5; Heb. 11:6
[2] Lev. 18:4; 1 Sam. 15:22; Eph. 2:10
[3] 1 Cor. 10:31
[4] Deut. 12:32; Isa. 29:13; Ezek. 20:18-19; Matt. 15:7-9

The Ten Commandments

LORD'S DAY 34

92 Q. What is God's law?
A. God spoke all these words:

THE FIRST COMMANDMENT
"I am the LORD your God,
who brought you out of the land of Egypt,
out of the house of slavery;
you shall have no other gods before me."

THE SECOND COMMANDMENT
"You shall not make for yourself an idol,
whether in the form of anything that is in heaven above,
or that is on the earth beneath,
or that is in the water under the earth.

You shall not bow down to them or worship them;
for I the Lord your God am a jealous God,
punishing children for the iniquity of parents,
to the third and the fourth generation
of those who reject me,
but showing love to the thousandth generation of those
who love me and keep my commandments."

THE THIRD COMMANDMENT
"You shall not make wrongful use of the name of the Lord your God,
for the Lord will not acquit anyone
who misuses his name."

THE FOURTH COMMANDMENT
"Remember the sabbath day, and keep it holy.
Six days you shall labor and do all your work.
But the seventh day is a sabbath to the Lord your God;
you shall not do any work—
you, your son or your daughter,
your male or female slave,
your livestock,
or the alien resident in your towns.
For in six days the Lord made
heaven and earth, the sea,
and all that is in them,
but rested the seventh day;
therefore the Lord blessed the sabbath day
and consecrated it."

THE FIFTH COMMANDMENT
"Honor your father and your mother,
so that your days may be long
in the land that the Lord your God is giving to you."

THE SIXTH COMMANDMENT
"You shall not murder."

THE SEVENTH COMMANDMENT
"You shall not commit adultery."

THE EIGHTH COMMANDMENT
"You shall not steal."

THE NINTH COMMANDMENT
"You shall not bear false witness
against your neighbor."

THE TENTH COMMANDMENT

"You shall not covet your neighbor's house;
you shall not covet your neighbor's wife,
> or male or female slave,
> or ox, or donkey,
> or anything that belongs to your neighbor."[1]

[1] Ex. 20:1-17; Deut. 5:6-21

93 Q. How are these commandments divided?

A. Into two tables.
The first has four commandments,
> teaching us how we ought to live in relation to God.
The second has six commandments,
> teaching us what we owe our neighbor.[1]

[1] Matt. 22:37-39

**94 Q. What does the Lord require
in the first commandment?**

A. That I, not wanting to endanger my own salvation,
avoid and shun
> all idolatry,[1] sorcery, superstitious rites,[2]
> and prayer to saints or to other creatures.[3]

That I rightly know the only true God,[4]
> trust him alone,[5]
> and look to God for every good thing[6]
> > humbly[7] and patiently,[8]
> and love,[9] fear,[10] and honor[11] God
> > with all my heart.
In short,
> that I give up anything
> rather than go against God's will in any way.[12]

[1] 1 Cor. 6:9-10; 10:5-14; 1 John 5:21
[2] Lev. 19:31; Deut. 18:9-12
[3] Matt. 4:10; Rev. 19:10; 22:8-9
[4] John 17:3
[5] Jer. 17:5, 7
[6] Ps. 104:27-28; James 1:17
[7] 1 Pet. 5:5-6
[8] Col. 1:11; Heb. 10:36
[9] Matt. 22:37 (Deut. 6:5)
[10] Prov. 9:10; 1 Pet. 1:17
[11] Matt. 4:10 (Deut. 6:13)
[12] Matt. 5:29-30; 10:37-39

95 **Q.** **What is idolatry?**

A. Idolatry is
having or inventing something in which one trusts
in place of or alongside of the only true God,
who has revealed himself in the Word.[1]

[1] 1 Chron. 16:26; Gal. 4:8-9; Eph. 5:5; Phil. 3:19

LORD'S DAY 35

96 **Q.** **What is God's will for us**
in the second commandment?

A. That we in no way make any image of God[1]
nor worship him in any other way
than has been commanded in God's Word.[2]

[1] Deut. 4:15-19; Isa. 40:18-25; Acts 17:29; Rom. 1:22-23
[2] Lev. 10:1-7; 1 Sam. 15:22-23; John 4:23-24

97 **Q.** **May we then not make**
any image at all?

A. God can not and may not
be visibly portrayed in any way.

Although creatures may be portrayed,
yet God forbids making or having such images
if one's intention is to worship them
or to serve God through them.[1]

[1] Ex. 34:13-14, 17; 2 Kings 18:4-5

98 **Q.** **But may not images be permitted in churches**
in place of books for the unlearned?

A. No, we should not try to be wiser than God.
God wants the Christian community instructed
by the living preaching of his Word—[1]
not by idols that cannot even talk.[2]

[1] Rom. 10:14-15, 17; 2 Tim. 3:16-17; 2 Pet. 1:19
[2] Jer. 10:8; Hab. 2:18-20

99 Q. **What is the aim of the third commandment?**
    A. That we neither blaspheme nor misuse the name of God
         by cursing,[1] perjury,[2] or unnecessary oaths,[3]
      nor share in such horrible sins
         by being silent bystanders.[4]

      In summary,
         we should use the holy name of God
            only with reverence and awe,[5]
         so that we may properly
            confess God,[6]
            pray to God,[7]
            and glorify God in all our words and works.[8]

[1] Lev. 24:10-17
[2] Lev. 19:12
[3] Matt. 5:37; James 5:12
[4] Lev. 5:1; Prov. 29:24
[5] Ps. 99:1-5; Jer. 4:2
[6] Matt. 10:32-33; Rom. 10:9-10
[7] Ps. 50:14-15; 1 Tim. 2:8
[8] Col. 3:17

100 Q. **Is blasphemy of God's name by swearing and cursing**
      really such serious sin
      that God is angry also with those
      who do not do all they can
      to help prevent and forbid it?
    A. Yes, indeed.[1]
         No sin is greater
         or provokes God's wrath more
         than blaspheming his name.
      That is why God commanded it to be punished with death.[2]

[1] Lev. 5:1
[2] Lev. 24:10-17

101 Q. **But may we swear an oath in God's name**
      if we do it reverently?
    A. Yes, when the government demands it,
      or when necessity requires it,
         in order to maintain and promote truth and trustworthiness
         for God's glory and our neighbor's good.

Such oaths are grounded in God's Word[1]
and were rightly used by the people of God
in the Old and New Testaments.[2]

[1] Deut. 6:13; 10:20; Jer. 4:1-2; Heb. 6:16
[2] Gen. 21:24; Josh. 9:15; 1 Kings 1:29-30; Rom. 1:9; 2 Cor. 1:23

102 Q. May we also swear by saints or other creatures?
    A. No.
        A legitimate oath means calling upon God
        as the only one who knows my heart
            to witness to my truthfulness
            and to punish me if I swear falsely.[1]
        No creature is worthy of such honor.[2]

[1] Rom. 9:1; 2 Cor. 1:23
[2] Matt. 5:34-37; 23:16-22; James 5:12

LORD'S DAY 38

**103 Q. What is God's will for you
      in the fourth commandment?**
    A. First,
        that the gospel ministry and education for it be maintained,[1]
        and that, especially on the festive day of rest,
        I diligently attend the assembly of God's people[2]
            to learn what God's Word teaches,[3]
            to participate in the sacraments,[4]
            to pray to God publicly,[5]
            and to bring Christian offerings for the poor.[6]

        Second,
            that every day of my life
                I rest from my evil ways,
                let the Lord work in me through his Spirit,
            and so begin in this life
                the eternal Sabbath.[7]

[1] Deut. 6:4-9, 20-25; 1 Cor. 9:13-14; 2 Tim. 2:2; 3:13-17; Tit. 1:5
[2] Deut. 12:5-12; Ps. 40:9-10; 68:26; Acts 2:42-47; Heb. 10:23-25
[3] Rom. 10:14-17; 1 Cor. 14:31-32; 1 Tim. 4:13
[4] 1 Cor. 11:23-25
[5] Col. 3:16; 1 Tim. 2:1
[6] Ps. 50:14; 1 Cor. 16:2; 2 Cor. 8 & 9
[7] Isa. 66:23; Heb. 4:9-11

**104 Q. What is God's will for you
in the fifth commandment?**

    A. That I honor, love, and be loyal
         to my father and mother
         and all those in authority over me;
      that I submit myself with proper obedience
         to all their good teaching and discipline;[1]
      and also that I be patient with their failings—[2]
      for through them God chooses to rule us.[3]

[1] Ex. 21:17; Prov. 1:8; 4:1; Rom. 13:1-2; Eph. 5:21-22; 6:1-9; Col. 3:18- 4:1
[2] Prov. 20:20; 23:22; 1 Pet. 2:18
[3] Matt. 22:21; Rom. 13:1-8; Eph. 6:1-9; Col. 3:18-21

**105 Q. What is God's will for you
in the sixth commandment?**

    A. I am not to belittle, hate, insult, or kill my neighbor—
         not by my thoughts, my words, my look or gesture,
         and certainly not by actual deeds—
      and I am not to be party to this in others;[1]
      rather, I am to put away all desire for revenge.[2]

      I am not to harm or recklessly endanger myself either.[3]
      Prevention of murder is also why
         government is armed with the sword.[4]

[1] Gen. 9:6; Lev. 19:17-18; Matt. 5:21-22; 26:52
[2] Prov. 25:21-22; Matt. 18:35; Rom. 12:19; Eph. 4:26
[3] Matt. 4:7; 26:52; Rom. 13:11-14
[4] Gen. 9:6; Ex. 21:14; Rom. 13:4

106 Q. Does this commandment refer only to murder?

    A. By forbidding murder God teaches us
         that he hates the root of murder:
         envy, hatred, anger, vindictiveness.[1]

      In God's sight all such are disguised forms of murder.[2]

[1] Prov. 14:30; Rom. 1:29; 12:19; Gal. 5:19-21; 1 John 2:9-11
[2] 1 John 3:15

107 Q. **Is it enough then**
that we do not murder our neighbor
in any such way?

A. No.
By condemning envy, hatred, and anger
God wants us
to love our neighbors as ourselves,[1]
to be patient, peace-loving, gentle,
merciful, and friendly toward them,[2]
to protect them from harm as much as we can,
and to do good even to our enemies.[3]

[1] Matt. 7:12; 22:39; Rom. 12:10
[2] Matt. 5:3-12; Luke 6:36; Rom. 12:10, 18; Gal. 6:1-2; Eph. 4:2; Col. 3:12; 1 Pet. 3:8
[3] Ex. 23:4-5; Matt. 5:44-45; Rom. 12:20-21 (Prov. 25:21-22)

LORD'S DAY 41

108 Q. **What does the seventh commandment teach us?**

A. That God condemns all unchastity,[1]
and that therefore we should thoroughly detest it[2]
and live decent and chaste lives,[3]
within or outside of the holy state of marriage.

[1] Lev. 18:30; Eph. 5:3-5
[2] Jude 22-23
[3] 1 Cor. 7:1-9; 1 Thess. 4:3-8; Heb. 13:4

109 Q. **Does God, in this commandment,**
forbid only such scandalous sins as adultery?

A. We are temples of the Holy Spirit, body and soul,
and God wants both to be kept clean and holy.
That is why God forbids
all unchaste actions, looks, talk, thoughts, or desires,[1]
and whatever may incite someone to them.[2]

[1] Matt. 5:27-29; 1 Cor. 6:18-20; Eph. 5:3-4
[2] 1 Cor. 15:33; Eph. 5:18

LORD'S DAY 42

110 Q. **What does God forbid**
in the eighth commandment?

A. God forbids not only outright theft and robbery,
punishable by law.[1]

But in God's sight theft also includes

all scheming and swindling
in order to get our neighbor's goods for ourselves,
　whether by force or means that appear legitimate,[2]
　such as
　　inaccurate measurements of weight, size, or volume;
　　fraudulent merchandising;
　　counterfeit money;
　　excessive interest;
　　or any other means forbidden by God.[3]

In addition God forbids all greed[4]
and pointless squandering of his gifts.[5]

[1] Ex. 22:1; 1 Cor. 5:9-10; 6:9-10
[2] Mic. 6:9-11; Luke 3:14; James 5:1-6
[3] Deut. 25:13-16; Ps. 15:5; Prov. 11:1; 12:22; Ezek. 45:9-12; Luke 6:35
[4] Luke 12:15; Eph. 5:5
[5] Prov. 21:20; 23:20-21; Luke 16:10-13

**111 Q. What does God require of you
in this commandment?**

A. That I do whatever I can
　for my neighbor's good,
that I treat others
　as I would like them to treat me,
and that I work faithfully
　so that I may share with those in need.[1]

[1] Isa. 58:5-10; Matt. 7:12; Gal. 6:9-10; Eph. 4:28

LORD'S DAY 43

112 Q. What is the aim of the ninth commandment?

A. That I
　never give false testimony against anyone,
　twist no one's words,
　not gossip or slander,
　nor join in condemning anyone
　rashly or without a hearing.[1]

Rather, in court and everywhere else,
I should avoid lying and deceit of every kind;
　these are the very devices the devil uses,
　and they would call down on me God's intense wrath.[2]
I should love the truth,
　speak it candidly,
　and openly acknowledge it.[3]

And I should do what I can
  to guard and advance my neighbor's good name.[4]

[1] Ps. 15; Prov. 19:5; Matt. 7:1; Luke 6:37; Rom. 1:28-32
[2] Lev. 19:11-12; Prov. 12:22; 13:5; John 8:44; Rev. 21:8
[3] 1 Cor. 13:6; Eph. 4:25
[4] 1 Pet. 3:8-9; 4:8

LORD'S DAY 44

113 Q. What is the aim of the tenth commandment?
 A. That not even the slightest desire or thought
   contrary to any one of God's commandments
   should ever arise in our hearts.

   Rather, with all our hearts
   we should always hate sin
   and take pleasure in whatever is right.[1]

[1] Ps. 19:7-14; 139:23-24; Rom. 7:7-8

114 Q. But can those converted to God
  obey these commandments perfectly?
 A. No.
  In this life even the holiest
  have only a small beginning of this obedience.[1]

  Nevertheless, with all seriousness of purpose,
  they do begin to live
  according to all, not only some,
  of God's commandments.[2]

[1] Eccles. 7:20; Rom. 7:14-15; 1 Cor. 13:9; 1 John 1:8-10
[2] Ps. 1:1-2; Rom. 7:22-25; Phil. 3:12-16

115 Q. Since no one in this life
  can obey the Ten Commandments perfectly,
  why does God want them
  preached so pointedly?
 A. First, so that the longer we live
   the more we may come to know our sinfulness
   and the more eagerly look to Christ
    for forgiveness of sins and righteousness.[1]

Second, so that
we may never stop striving,
and never stop praying to God for the grace of the Holy Spirit,
to be renewed more and more after God's image,
until after this life we reach our goal:
perfection.[2]

[1] Ps. 32:5; Rom. 3:19-26; 7:7, 24-25; 1 John 1:9
[2] 1 Cor. 9:24; Phil. 3:12-14; 1 John 3:1-3

The Lord's Prayer

LORD'S DAY 45

116 Q. Why do Christians need to pray?

　　A. Because prayer is the most important part
of the thankfulness God requires of us.[1]
And also because God gives his grace and Holy Spirit
only to those who pray continually and groan inwardly,
asking God for these gifts
and thanking God for them.[2]

[1] Ps. 50:14-15; 116:12-19; 1 Thess. 5:16-18
[2] Matt. 7:7-8; Luke 11:9-13

**117 Q. What is the kind of prayer
that pleases God and that he listens to?**

　　A. First, we must pray from the heart
to no other than the one true God,
revealed to us in his Word,
asking for everything God has commanded us to ask for.[1]

Second, we must fully recognize our need and misery,
so that we humble ourselves in God's majestic presence.[2]

Third, we must rest on this unshakable foundation:
even though we do not deserve it,
God will surely listen to our prayer
because of Christ our Lord.
That is what God promised us in his Word.[3]

[1] Ps. 145:18-20; John 4:22-24; Rom. 8:26-27; James 1:5; 1 John 5:14-15
[2] 2 Chron. 7:14; Ps. 2:11; 34:18; 62:8; Isa. 66:2; Rev. 4
[3] Dan. 9:17-19; Matt. 7:8; John 14:13-14; 16:23; Rom. 10:13; James 1:6

118 Q. **What did God command us to pray for?**

A. Everything we need, spiritually and physically,[1]
as embraced in the prayer
Christ our Lord himself taught us.

[1] James 1:17; Matt. 6:33

119 Q. **What is this prayer?**

A. Our Father in heaven,
hallowed be your name.
Your kingdom come.
Your will be done,
    on earth as it is in heaven.
Give us this day our daily bread.
And forgive us our debts,
    as we also have forgiven our debtors.
And do not bring us to the time of trial,
    but rescue us from the evil one.*
For the kingdom
    and the power
    and the glory are yours forever.
Amen.[1]**

[1] Matt. 6:9-13; Luke 11:2-4
*This text of the Lord's Prayer is from the New Revised Standard Version in keeping with the use of the NRSV throughout this edition of the catechism. Most biblical scholars agree that it is an accurate translation of the Greek text and carries virtually the same meaning as the more traditional text of the Lord's Prayer.
**Earlier and better manuscripts of Matthew 6 omit the words "For the kingdom and . . . Amen."

LORD'S DAY 46

120 Q. **Why did Christ command us**
to call God "our Father"?

A. To awaken in us
at the very beginning of our prayer
what should be basic to our prayer—
    a childlike reverence and trust
    that through Christ God has become our Father,
and that just as our parents do not refuse us
    the things of this life,
even less will God our Father refuse to give us
    what we ask in faith.[1]

[1] Matt. 7:9-11; Luke 11:11-13

121 Q. **Why the words**
"in heaven"?

   A. These words teach us
      not to think of God's heavenly majesty
         as something earthly,[1]
      and to expect everything
         needed for body and soul
         from God's almighty power.[2]

[1] Jer. 23:23-24; Acts 17:24-25
[2] Matt. 6:25-34; Rom. 8:31-32

LORD'S DAY 47

122 Q. **What does the first petition mean?**

   A. "Hallowed be your name" means:

      Help us to truly know you,[1]
      to honor, glorify, and praise you
         for all your works
         and for all that shines forth from them:
            your almighty power, wisdom, kindness,
            justice, mercy, and truth.[2]

      And it means,

      Help us to direct all our living—
         what we think, say, and do—
      so that your name will never be blasphemed because of us
      but always honored and praised.[3]

[1] Jer. 9:23-24; 31:33-34; Matt. 16:17; John 17:3
[2] Ex. 34:5-8; Ps. 145; Jer. 32:16-20; Luke 1:46-55, 68-75; Rom. 11:33-36
[3] Ps. 115:1; Matt. 5:16

LORD'S DAY 48

123 Q. **What does the second petition mean?**

   A. "Your kingdom come" means:
      Rule us by your Word and Spirit in such a way
         that more and more we submit to you.[1]

      Preserve your church and make it grow.[2]

      Destroy the devil's work;
      destroy every force which revolts against you
      and every conspiracy against your holy Word.[3]

Do this until your kingdom fully comes,
    when you will be
        all in all.[4]

[1] Ps. 119:5, 105; 143:10; Matt. 6:33
[2] Ps. 122:6-9; Matt. 16:18; Acts 2:42-47
[3] Rom. 16:20; 1 John 3:8
[4] Rom. 8:22-23; 1 Cor. 15:28; Rev. 22:17, 20

LORD'S DAY 49

124 Q. What does the third petition mean?
    A. "Your will be done, on earth as it is in heaven" means:

Help us and all people
    to reject our own wills
    and to obey your will without any back talk.
    Your will alone is good.[1]

Help us one and all to carry out the work we are called to,[2]
    as willingly and faithfully as the angels in heaven.[3]

[1] Matt. 7:21; 16:24-26; Luke 22:42; Rom. 12:1-2; Tit. 2:11-12
[2] 1 Cor. 7:17-24; Eph. 6:5-9
[3] Ps. 103:20-21

LORD'S DAY 50

125 Q. What does the fourth petition mean?
    A. "Give us this day our daily bread" means:

Do take care of all our physical needs[1]
so that we come to know
    that you are the only source of everything good,[2]
    and that neither our work and worry
    nor your gifts
    can do us any good without your blessing.[3]

And so help us to give up our trust in creatures
    and trust in you alone.[4]

[1] Ps. 104:27-30; 145:15-16; Matt. 6:25-34
[2] Acts 14:17; 17:25; James 1:17
[3] Deut. 8:3; Ps. 37:16; 127:1-2; 1 Cor. 15:58
[4] Ps. 55:22; 62; 146; Jer. 17:5-8; Heb. 13:5-6

126 Q. What does the fifth petition mean?

A. "Forgive us our debts,
as we also have forgiven our debtors" means:

Because of Christ's blood,
do not hold against us, poor sinners that we are,
any of the sins we do
or the evil that constantly clings to us.[1]

Forgive us just as we are fully determined,
as evidence of your grace in us,
to forgive our neighbors.[2]

[1] Ps. 51:1-7; 143:2; Rom. 8:1; 1 John 2:1-2
[2] Matt. 6:14-15; 18:21-35

---

127 Q. What does the sixth petition mean?

A. "And do not bring us to the time of trial,
but rescue us from the evil one" means:

By ourselves we are too weak
to hold our own even for a moment.[1]
And our sworn enemies—
the devil,[2] the world,[3] and our own flesh—[4]
never stop attacking us.

And so, Lord,
uphold us and make us strong
with the strength of your Holy Spirit,
so that we may not go down to defeat
in this spiritual struggle,[5]
but may firmly resist our enemies
until we finally win the complete victory.[6]

[1] Ps. 103:14-16; John 15:1-5
[2] 2 Cor. 11:14; Eph. 6:10-13; 1 Pet. 5:8
[3] John 15:18-21
[4] Rom. 7:23; Gal. 5:17
[5] Matt. 10:19-20; 26:41; Mark 13:33; Rom. 5:3-5
[6] 1 Cor. 10:13; 1 Thess. 3:13; 5:23

128 Q. What does your conclusion to this prayer mean?

    A. "For the kingdom
and the power
and the glory are yours forever" means:

We have made all these petitions of you
because, as our all-powerful king,
    you are both willing and able
    to give us all that is good;[1]
and because your holy name,
    and not we ourselves,
should receive all the praise, forever.[2]

[1] Rom. 10:11-13; 2 Pet. 2:9
[2] Ps. 115:1; John 14:13

129 Q. What does that little word "Amen" express?

    A. "Amen" means:

This shall truly and surely be!

It is even more sure
    that God listens to my prayer
than that I really desire
    what I pray for.[1]

[1] Isa. 65:24; 2 Cor. 1:20; 2 Tim. 2:13

The Canons of Dort

Introduction

The Decision of the Synod of Dort on the Five Main Points of Doctrine in Dispute in the Netherlands is popularly known as the Canons of Dort. It consists of statements of doctrine adopted by the great Synod of Dort, which met in the city of Dordrecht in 1618-19. Although this was a national synod of the Reformed churches of the Netherlands, it had an international character, since it was composed not only of Dutch delegates but also of twenty-six delegates from eight foreign countries.

The Synod of Dort was held in order to settle a serious controversy in the Dutch churches initiated by the rise of Arminianism. Jacob Arminius, a theological professor at Leiden University, questioned the teaching of Calvin and his followers on a number of important points. After Arminius's death, his own followers presented their views on five of these points in the Remonstrance of 1610. In this document and in later more explicit writings, the Arminians taught election based on foreseen faith, the universal application of Christ's atonement available to all who freely choose to accept it, limited human depravity, the resistibility of God's grace, and the possibility of a fall from salvation. In the Canons the Synod of Dort rejected these views and set forth the Reformed teaching on these points with the purpose of offering a deeper assurance of salvation to believers in accordance with the teaching of the Scriptures.

The Canons are thus unique among the Reformed confessions because of their original purpose as a judicial decision on the doctrinal points in dispute during the Arminian controversy. The original preface called them a "judgment, in which both the true view, agreeing with God's Word, concerning the aforesaid five points of doctrine, is explained, and the false view, disagreeing with God's Word, is rejected." The Canons also have a narrower scope than the Belgic Confession and the Heidelberg Catechism in that they do not cover the whole range of doctrine but focus on the five points of doctrine in dispute.

Although in form there are only four points in the Canons of Dort, we speak properly of five points, because the Canons were structured to correspond to the five articles of the 1610 Remonstrance. Main Points Three and Four were combined into one, always designated as Main Point Three/Four. Each of the main points consists of a positive and a negative part, the former being an exposition of the Reformed doctrine on the subject, the latter a repudiation of the corresponding errors. While the Reformed Church in America does not give confessional status to the Rejection of Errors, it nevertheless recognizes that the rejections help interpret the Canons by highlighting the specific errors addressed.

The biblical quotations in the Canons are translations from the original Latin and so do not always correspond to current versions. Though not in the original text, subheadings have been added to the positive articles and to the conclusion in order to facilitate study of the Canons.

The First Main Point of Doctrine
Divine Election and Reprobation

The Judgment Concerning Divine Predestination Which the Synod Declares to Be in Agreement with the Word of God and Accepted Till Now in the Reformed Churches, Set Forth in Several Articles

Article 1: God's Right to Condemn All People
Since all people have sinned in Adam and have come under the sentence of the curse and eternal death, God would have done no one an injustice if it had been his will to leave the entire human race in sin and under the curse, and to condemn them on account of their sin. As the apostle says: "The whole world is liable to the condemnation of God" (Rom. 3:19), "All have sinned and are deprived of the glory of God" (Rom. 3:23), and "The wages of sin is death" (Rom. 6:23).

Article 2: The Manifestation of God's Love
But this is how God showed his love: he sent his only begotten Son into the world, so that whoever believes in him should not perish but have eternal life (1 John 4:9; John 3:16).

Article 3: The Preaching of the Gospel
In order that people may be brought to faith, God mercifully sends messengers of this very joyful message to the people and at the time he wills. By this ministry people are called to repentance and faith in Christ crucified. For "how shall they believe in him of whom they have not heard? And how shall they hear without someone preaching? And how shall they preach unless they have been sent?" (Rom. 10:14-15).

Article 4: A Twofold Response to the Gospel
God's wrath remains on those who do not believe this gospel. But those who do accept it and embrace Jesus the Savior with a true and living faith are delivered through him from God's wrath and from destruction, and receive the gift of eternal life.

Article 5: The Sources of Unbelief and of Faith
The cause or blame for this unbelief, as well as for all other sins, is not at all in God, but in humanity. Faith in Jesus Christ, however, and salvation through him is a free gift of God. As Scripture says, "It is by grace you have been saved, through faith, and this not from yourselves; it is a gift of God" (Eph. 2:8). Likewise: "It has been freely given to you to believe in Christ" (Phil. 1:29).

Article 6: God's Eternal Decree
The fact that some receive from God the gift of faith within time, and that others do not, stems from his eternal decree. For "all his works are known to God from eternity" (Acts 15:18; Eph. 1:11). In accordance with this decree

God graciously softens the hearts, however hard, of the elect and inclines them to believe, but by a just judgment God leaves in their wickedness and hardness of heart those who have not been chosen. And in this especially is disclosed to us God's act—unfathomable, and as merciful as it is just—of distinguishing between people equally lost. This is the well-known decree of election and reprobation revealed in God's Word. The wicked, impure, and unstable distort this decree to their own ruin, but it provides holy and godly souls with comfort beyond words.

Article 7: Election
Election is God's unchangeable purpose by which he did the following:

Before the foundation of the world, by sheer grace, according to the free good pleasure of his will, God chose in Christ to salvation a definite number of particular people out of the entire human race, which had fallen by its own fault from its original innocence into sin and ruin. Those chosen were neither better nor more deserving than the others, but lay with them in the common misery. God did this in Christ, whom he also appointed from eternity to be the mediator, the head of all those chosen, and the foundation of their salvation.

And so God decreed to give to Christ those chosen for salvation, and to call and draw them effectively into Christ's fellowship through the Word and Spirit. In other words, God decreed to grant them true faith in Christ, to justify them, to sanctify them, and finally, after powerfully preserving them in the fellowship of the Son, to glorify them.

God did all this in order to demonstrate his mercy, to the praise of the riches of God's glorious grace.

As Scripture says, "God chose us in Christ, before the foundation of the world, so that we should be holy and blameless before him with love; he predestined us whom he adopted as his children through Jesus Christ, in himself, according to the good pleasure of his will, to the praise of his glorious grace, by which he freely made us pleasing to himself in his beloved" (Eph. 1:4-6). And elsewhere, "Those whom he predestined, he also called; and those whom he called, he also justified; and those whom he justified, he also glorified" (Rom. 8:30).

Article 8: A Single Decree of Election
This election is not of many kinds, but one and the same for all who were to be saved in the Old and the New Testament. For Scripture declares that there is a single good pleasure, purpose, and plan of God's will, by which he chose us from eternity both to grace and to glory, both to salvation and to the way of salvation, which God prepared in advance for us to walk in.

Article 9: Election Not Based on Foreseen Faith

This same election took place, not on the basis of foreseen faith, of the obedience of faith, of holiness, or of any other good quality and disposition, as though it were based on a prerequisite cause or condition in the person to be chosen, but rather for the purpose of faith, of the obedience of faith, of holiness, and so on. Accordingly, election is the source of every saving good. Faith, holiness, and the other saving gifts, and at last eternal life itself, flow forth from election as its fruits and effects. As the apostle says, "He chose us" (not because we were, but) "so that we should be holy and blameless before him in love" (Eph. 1:4).

Article 10: Election Based on God's Good Pleasure

But the cause of this undeserved election is exclusively the good pleasure of God. This does not involve God's choosing certain human qualities or actions from among all those possible as a condition of salvation, but rather involves adopting certain particular persons from among the common mass of sinners as God's own possession. As Scripture says, "When the children were not yet born, and had done nothing either good or bad . . . , she (Rebecca) was told, 'The older will serve the younger.' As it is written, 'Jacob I loved, but Esau I hated'" (Rom. 9:11-13). Also, "All who were appointed for eternal life believed" (Acts 13:48).

Article 11: Election Unchangeable

Just as God is most wise, unchangeable, all-knowing, and almighty, so the election made by him can neither be suspended nor altered, revoked, or annulled; neither can God's chosen ones be cast off, nor their number reduced.

Article 12: The Assurance of Election

Assurance of their eternal and unchangeable election to salvation is given to the chosen in due time, though by various stages and in differing measure. Such assurance comes not by inquisitive searching into the hidden and deep things of God, but by noticing within themselves, with spiritual joy and holy delight, the unmistakable fruits of election pointed out in God's Word—such as a true faith in Christ, a childlike fear of God, a godly sorrow for their sins, a hunger and thirst for righteousness, and so on.

Article 13: The Fruit of This Assurance

In their awareness and assurance of this election, God's children daily find greater cause to humble themselves before God, to adore the fathomless depth of God's mercies, to cleanse themselves, and to give fervent love in return to the One who first so greatly loved them. This is far from saying that this teaching concerning election, and reflection upon it, make God's children lax in observing his commandments or carnally self-assured. By God's just judgment this does usually happen to those who casually take for granted the grace of election or engage in idle and brazen talk about it but are unwilling to walk in the ways of the chosen.

plan, this teaching concerning divine election was proclaimed
prophets, Christ himself, and the apostles, in Old and New Testimes. It was subsequently committed to writing in the Holy Scriptures. So also today in God's church, for which it was specifically intended, this teaching must be set forth with a spirit of discretion, in a godly and holy manner, at the appropriate time and place, without inquisitive searching into the ways of the Most High. This must be done for the glory of God's most holy name, and for the lively comfort of God's people.

Article 15: Reprobation

Moreover, Holy Scripture most especially highlights this eternal and undeserved grace of our election and brings it out more clearly for us, in that it further bears witness that not all people have been chosen but that some have not been chosen or have been passed by in God's eternal election—those, that is, concerning whom God, on the basis of his entirely free, most just, irreproachable, and unchangeable good pleasure, made the following decree:

> to leave them in the common misery into which, by their own fault, they have plunged themselves; not to grant them saving faith and the grace of conversion; but finally to condemn and eternally punish those who have been left in their own ways and under God's just judgment, not only for their unbelief but also for all their other sins, in order to display his justice.

And this is the decree of reprobation, which does not at all make God the author of sin (a blasphemous thought!) but rather its fearful, irreproachable, just judge and avenger.

Article 16: Responses to the Teaching of Reprobation

Those who do not yet actively experience within themselves a living faith in Christ or an assured confidence of heart, peace of conscience, a zeal for childlike obedience, and a glorying in God through Christ, but who nevertheless use the means by which God has promised to work these things in us—such people ought not to be alarmed at the mention of reprobation, nor to count themselves among the reprobate; rather they ought to continue diligently in the use of the means, to desire fervently a time of more abundant grace, and to wait for it in reverence and humility. On the other hand, those who seriously desire to turn to God, to be pleasing to God alone, and to be delivered from the body of death, but are not yet able to make such progress along the way of godliness and faith as they would like—such people ought much less to stand in fear of the teaching concerning reprobation, since our merciful God has promised not to snuff out a smoldering wick or break a bruised reed.* However, those who have forgotten God and their Savior Jesus Christ and have abandoned themselves wholly to the cares of the world and the pleasures of the flesh—such people have every reason to stand in fear of this teaching, as long as they do not seriously turn to God.

*Isaiah 42:3

Article 17: The Salvation of the Infants of Believers

Since we must make judgments about God's will from his Word, which t. fies that the children of believers are holy, not by nature but by virtue of ti gracious covenant in which they together with their parents are included, godly parents ought not to doubt the election and salvation of their children whom God calls out of this life in infancy.

Article 18: The Proper Attitude Toward Election and Reprobation

To those who complain about this grace of an undeserved election and about the severity of a just reprobation, we reply with the words of the apostle, "Who are you, O man, to talk back to God?" (Rom. 9:20), and with the words of our Savior, "Have I no right to do what I want with my own?" (Matt. 20:15). We, however, with reverent adoration of these secret things, cry out with the apostle: "Oh, the depths of the riches both of the wisdom and the knowledge of God! How unsearchable are his judgments, and his ways beyond tracing out! For who has known the mind of the Lord? Or who has been his counselor? Or who has first given to God, that God should repay him? For from him and through him and to him are all things. To him be the glory forever! Amen" (Rom. 11:33-36).

Rejection of the Errors by Which the Dutch Churches Have for Some Time Been Disturbed

Having set forth the orthodox teaching concerning election and reprobation, the Synod rejects the errors of those

I

Who teach that the will of God to save those who would believe and persevere in faith and in the obedience of faith is the whole and entire decision of election to salvation, and that nothing else concerning this decision has been revealed in God's Word.

For they deceive the simple and plainly contradict Holy Scripture in its testimony that God does not only wish to save those who would believe, but that he has also from eternity chosen certain particular people to whom, rather than to others, he would within time grant faith in Christ and perseverance. As Scripture says, "I have revealed your name to those whom you gave me" (John 17:6). Likewise, "All who were appointed for eternal life believed" (Acts 13:48), and "He chose us before the foundation of the world so that we should be holy . . ." (Eph. 1:4).

II

Who teach that God's election to eternal life is of many kinds: one general and indefinite, the other particular and definite; and the latter in turn either incomplete, revocable, conditional, or else complete, irrevocable, and absolute. Likewise, who teach that there is one election to faith and another to salvation, so that there can be an election to justifying faith apart from a nonconditional election to salvation.

n invention of the human mind, devised apart from the Scrip-
distorts the teaching concerning election and breaks up this
ain of salvation: "Those whom he predestined, he also called; and
vhom he called, he also justified; and those whom he justified, he also
ified" (Rom. 8:30).

III

Who teach that God's good pleasure and purpose, which Scripture mentions in its teaching of election, does not involve God's choosing certain particular people rather than others, but involves God's choosing, out of all possible conditions (including the works of the law) or out of the whole order of things, the intrinsically unworthy act of faith, as well as the imperfect obedience of faith, to be a condition of salvation; and it involves his graciously wishing to count this as perfect obedience and to look upon it as worthy of the reward of eternal life.

For by this pernicious error the good pleasure of God and the merit of Christ are robbed of their effectiveness and people are drawn away, by unprofitable inquiries, from the truth of undeserved justification and from the simplicity of the Scriptures. It also gives the lie to these words of the apostle: "God called us with a holy calling, not in virtue of works, but in virtue of his own purpose and the grace which was given to us in Christ Jesus before the beginning of time" (2 Tim. 1:9).

IV

Who teach that in election to faith a prerequisite condition is that humans should rightly use the light of nature, be upright, unassuming, humble, and disposed to eternal life, as though election depended to some extent on these factors.

For this smacks of Pelagius, and it clearly calls into question the words of the apostle: "We lived at one time in the passions of our flesh, following the will of our flesh and thoughts, and we were by nature children of wrath, like everyone else. But God, who is rich in mercy, out of the great love with which he loved us, even when we were dead in transgressions, made us alive with Christ, by whose grace you have been saved. And God raised us up with him and seated us with him in heaven in Christ Jesus, in order that in the coming ages we might show the surpassing riches of his grace, according to his kindness toward us in Christ Jesus. For it is by grace you have been saved, through faith (and this not from yourselves; it is the gift of God) not by works, so that no one can boast" (Eph. 2:3-9).

V

Who teach that the incomplete and conditional election of particular persons to salvation occurred on the basis of a foreseen faith, repentance, holiness, and godliness, which has just begun or continued for some time; but that complete and nonconditional election occurred on the basis of a

foreseen perseverance to the end in faith, repentance, holiness, anc̣
ness. And that this is the gracious and evangelical worthiness, on acc̣
of which the one who is chosen is more worthy than the one who is ,
chosen. And therefore that faith, the obedience of faith, holiness, godlineṣ
and perseverance are not fruits or effects of an unchangeable election to
glory, but indispensable conditions and causes, which are prerequisite in
those who are to be chosen in the complete election, and which are foreseen
as achieved in them.

This runs counter to the entire Scripture, which throughout impresses upon
our ears and hearts these sayings among others: "Election is not by works,
but by him who calls" (Rom. 9:11-12); "All who were appointed for eternal
life believed" (Acts 13:48); "He chose us in himself so that we should be
holy" (Eph. 1:4); "You did not choose me, but I chose you" (John 15:16);
"If by grace, not by works" (Rom. 11:6); "In this is love, not that we loved
God, but that he loved us and sent his Son" (1 John 4:10).

VI
Who teach that not every election to salvation is unchangeable, but that
some of the chosen can perish and do in fact perish eternally, with no decision of God to prevent it.

By this gross error they make God changeable, destroy the comfort of the
godly concerning the steadfastness of their election, and contradict the
Holy Scriptures, which teach that "the elect cannot be led astray" (Matt.
24:24), that "Christ does not lose those given to him by the Father" (John
6:39), and that "those whom God predestined, called, and justified, he also
glorifies" (Rom. 8:30).

VII
Who teach that in this life there is no fruit, no awareness, and no assurance
of one's unchangeable election to glory, except as conditioned upon something changeable and contingent.

For not only is it absurd to speak of an uncertain assurance, but these things
also militate against the experience of the saints, who with the apostle
rejoice from an awareness of their election and sing the praises of this gift
of God; who, as Christ urged, "rejoice" with his disciples "that their names
have been written in heaven" (Luke 10:20); and finally who hold up against
the flaming arrows of the devil's temptations the awareness of their election,
with the question "Who will bring any charge against those whom God has
chosen?" (Rom. 8:33).

VIII
Who teach that it was not on the basis of his just will alone that God decided
to leave anyone in the fall of Adam and in the common state of sin and con-

r to pass anyone by in the imparting of grace necessary for faith
...on.

...words stand fast: "He has mercy on whom he wishes, and he hard-
...om he wishes" (Rom. 9:18). And also: "To you it has been given to
...w the secrets of the kingdom of heaven, but to them it has not been
...ven" (Matt. 13:11). Likewise: "I give glory to you, Father, Lord of heaven
and earth, that you have hidden these things from the wise and understanding, and have revealed them to little children; yes, Father, because that was
your pleasure" (Matt. 11:25-26).

IX
Who teach that the cause for God's sending the gospel to one people rather
than to another is not merely and solely God's good pleasure, but rather
that one people is better and worthier than the other to whom the gospel is
not communicated.

For Moses contradicts this when he addresses the people of Israel as follows:
"Behold, to Jehovah your God belong the heavens and the highest heavens,
the earth and whatever is in it. But Jehovah was inclined in his affection to
love your ancestors alone, and chose out their descendants after them, you
above all peoples, as at this day" (Deut. 10:14-15). And also Christ: "Woe to
you, Korazin! Woe to you, Bethsaida! for if those mighty works done in you
had been done in Tyre and Sidon, they would have repented long ago in
sackcloth and ashes" (Matt. 11:21).

The Second Main Point of Doctrine
Christ's Death and Human Redemption Through It

Article 1: The Punishment Which God's Justice Requires
God is not only supremely merciful, but also supremely just. This justice
requires (as God has revealed in the Word) that the sins we have committed against his infinite majesty be punished with both temporal and eternal
punishments, of soul as well as body. We cannot escape these punishments
unless satisfaction is given to God's justice.

Article 2: The Satisfaction Made by Christ
Since, however, we ourselves cannot give this satisfaction or deliver ourselves from God's wrath, God in boundless mercy has given us as a guarantee his only begotten Son, who was made to be sin and a curse for us, in our
place, on the cross, in order that he might give satisfaction for us.

Article 3: The Infinite Value of Christ's Death
This death of God's Son is the only and entirely complete sacrifice and satisfaction for sins; it is of infinite value and worth, more than sufficient to
atone for the sins of the whole world.

Article 4: Reasons for This Infinite Value
This death is of such great value and worth for the reason that the perso who suffered it is—as was necessary to be our Savior—not only a true an perfectly holy human, but also the only begotten Son of God, of the same eternal and infinite essence with the Father and the Holy Spirit. Another reason is that this death was accompanied by the experience of God's wrath and curse, which we by our sins had fully deserved.

Article 5: The Mandate to Proclaim the Gospel to All
Moreover, it is the promise of the gospel that whoever believes in Christ crucified shall not perish but have eternal life. This promise, together with the command to repent and believe, ought to be announced and declared without differentiation or discrimination to all nations and people, to whom God in his good pleasure sends the gospel.

Article 6: Unbelief, a Human Responsibility
However, that many who have been called through the gospel do not repent or believe in Christ but perish in unbelief is not because the sacrifice of Christ offered on the cross is deficient or insufficient, but because they themselves are at fault.

Article 7: Faith God's Gift
But all who genuinely believe and are delivered and saved by Christ's death from their sins and from destruction receive this favor solely from God's grace—which God owes to no one—given to them in Christ from eternity.

Article 8: The Saving Effectiveness of Christ's Death
For it was the entirely free plan and very gracious will and intention of God the Father that the enlivening and saving effectiveness of his Son's costly death should work itself out in all the elect, in order that God might grant justifying faith to them only and thereby lead them without fail to salvation. In other words, it was God's will that Christ through the blood of the cross (by which he confirmed the new covenant) should effectively redeem from every people, tribe, nation, and language all those and only those who were chosen from eternity to salvation and given to him by the Father; that Christ should grant them faith (which, like the Holy Spirit's other saving gifts, he acquired for them by his death). It was also God's will that Christ should cleanse them by his blood from all their sins, both original and actual, whether committed before or after their coming to faith; that he should faithfully preserve them to the very end; and that he should finally present them to himself, a glorious people, without spot or wrinkle.

Article 9: The Fulfillment of God's Plan
This plan, arising out of God's eternal love for the elect, from the beginning of the world to the present time has been powerfully carried out and will also be carried out in the future, the gates of hell seeking vainly to prevail against it. As a result, the elect are gathered into one, all in their own time, and there is always a church of believers founded on Christ's blood,

...h which steadfastly loves, persistently worships, and here and in all ...ty praises him as her Savior who laid down his life for her on the cross, ...bridegroom for his bride.

Rejection of the Errors

Having set forth the orthodox teaching, the Synod rejects the errors of those

I

Who teach that God the Father appointed his Son to death on the cross without a fixed and definite plan to save anyone by name, so that the necessity, usefulness, and worth of what Christ's death obtained could have stood intact and altogether perfect, complete and whole, even if the redemption that was obtained had never in actual fact been applied to any individual.

For this assertion is an insult to the wisdom of God the Father and to the merit of Jesus Christ, and it is contrary to Scripture. For the Savior speaks as follows: "I lay down my life for the sheep, and I know them" (John 10:15, 27). And Isaiah the prophet says concerning the Savior: "When he shall make himself an offering for sin, he shall see his offspring, he shall prolong his days, and the will of Jehovah shall prosper in his hand" (Isa. 53:10). Finally, this undermines the article of the creed in which we confess what we believe concerning the church.

II

Who teach that the purpose of Christ's death was not to establish in actual fact a new covenant of grace by his blood, but only to acquire for the Father the mere right to enter once more into a covenant with humanity, whether of grace or of works.

For this conflicts with Scripture, which teaches that Christ "has become the guarantee and mediator" of a better—that is, a new—covenant (Heb. 7:22; 9:15), "and that a will is in force only when someone has died" (Heb. 9:17).

III

Who teach that Christ, by the satisfaction which he gave, did not certainly merit for anyone salvation itself and the faith by which this satisfaction of Christ is effectively applied to salvation, but only acquired for the Father the authority or plenary will to relate in a new way with humanity and to impose such new conditions as he chose, and that the satisfying of these conditions depends on human free choice; consequently, that it was possible that either all or none would fulfill them.

For they have too low an opinion of the death of Christ, do not at all acknowledge the foremost fruit or benefit which it brings forth, and summon back from hell the Pelagian error.

IV

Who teach that what is involved in the new covenant of grace which God the Father made with humanity through the intervening of Christ's death is not that we are justified before God and saved through faith, insofar as it accepts Christ's merit, but rather that God, having withdrawn his demand for perfect obedience to the law, counts faith itself, and the imperfect obedience of faith, as perfect obedience to the law, and graciously looks upon this as worthy of the reward of eternal life.

For they contradict Scripture: "They are justified freely by his grace through the redemption that came by Jesus Christ, whom God presented as a sacrifice of atonement, through faith in his blood" (Rom. 3:24-25). And along with the ungodly Socinus, they introduce a new and foreign justification of humanity before God, against the consensus of the whole church.

V

Who teach that all people have been received into the state of reconciliation and into the grace of the covenant, so that no one on account of original sin is liable to condemnation, or is to be condemned, but that all are free from the guilt of this sin.

For this opinion conflicts with Scripture which asserts that we are by nature children of wrath.

VI

Who make use of the distinction between obtaining and applying in order to instill in the unwary and inexperienced the opinion that God, as far as he is concerned, wished to bestow equally upon all people the benefits which are gained by Christ's death; but that the distinction by which some rather than others come to share in the forgiveness of sins and eternal life depends on their own free choice (which applies itself to the grace offered indiscriminately) but does not depend on the unique gift of mercy which effectively works in them, so that they, rather than others, apply that grace to themselves.

For, while pretending to set forth this distinction in an acceptable sense, they attempt to give the people the deadly poison of Pelagianism.

VII

Who teach that Christ neither could die, nor had to die, nor did die for those whom God so dearly loved and chose to eternal life, since such people do not need the death of Christ.

For they contradict the apostle, who says: "Christ loved me and gave himself up for me" (Gal. 2:20), and likewise: "Who will bring any charge against those whom God has chosen? It is God who justifies. Who is he that condemns? It is Christ who died," that is, for them (Rom. 8:33-34). They also contradict the Savior, who asserts: "I lay down my life for the sheep"

(John 10:15), and "My command is this: Love one another as I have loved you. Greater love has no one than this, that one lay down his life for one's friends" (John 15:12-13).

The Third and Fourth Main Points of Doctrine
Human Corruption, Conversion to God, and the Way It Occurs

Article 1: The Effect of the Fall on Human Nature
Human beings were originally created in the image of God and were furnished in mind with a true and sound knowledge of the Creator and things spiritual, in will and heart with righteousness, and in all emotions with purity; indeed, the whole human being was holy. However, rebelling against God at the devil's instigation and by their own free will, they deprived themselves of these outstanding gifts. Rather, in their place they brought upon themselves blindness, terrible darkness, futility, and distortion of judgment in their minds; perversity, defiance, and hardness in their hearts and wills; and finally impurity in all their emotions.

Article 2: The Spread of Corruption
Human beings brought forth children of the same nature as themselves after the fall. That is to say, being corrupt they brought forth corrupt children. The
corruption spread, by God's just judgment, from Adam and Eve to all their descendants—except for Christ alone—not by way of imitation (as in former times the Pelagians would have it) but by way of the propagation of their perverted nature.

Article 3: Total Inability
Therefore, all people are conceived in sin and are born children of wrath, unfit for any saving good, inclined to evil, dead in their sins, and slaves to sin. Without the grace of the regenerating Holy Spirit they are neither willing nor able to return to God, to reform their distorted nature, or even to dispose themselves to such reform.

Article 4: The Inadequacy of the Light of Nature
There is, to be sure, a certain light of nature remaining in all people after the fall, by virtue of which they retain some notions about God, natural things, and the difference between what is moral and immoral, and demonstrate a certain eagerness for virtue and for good outward behavior. But this light of nature is far from enabling humans to come to a saving knowledge of God and conversion to him—so far, in fact, that they do not use it rightly even in matters of nature and society. Instead, in various ways they completely distort this light, whatever its precise character, and suppress it in unrighteousness. In doing so all people render themselves without excuse before God.

Article 5: The Inadequacy of the Law

In this respect, what is true of the light of nature is true also of the Ten Commandments given by God through Moses specifically to the Jews. For humans cannot obtain saving grace through the Decalogue, because, although it does expose the magnitude of their sin and increasingly convict them of their guilt, yet it does not offer a remedy or enable them to escape from human misery, and, indeed, weakened as it is by the flesh, leaves the offender under the curse.

Article 6: The Saving Power of the Gospel

What, therefore, neither the light of nature nor the law can do, God accomplishes by the power of the Holy Spirit, through the Word or the ministry of reconciliation. This is the gospel about the Messiah, through which it has pleased God to save believers, in both the Old and the New Testaments.

Article 7: God's Freedom in Revealing the Gospel

In the Old Testament, God revealed this secret of his will to a small number; in the New Testament (now without any distinction between peoples) God discloses it to a large number. The reason for this difference must not be ascribed to the greater worth of one nation over another, or to a better use of the light of nature, but to the free good pleasure and undeserved love of God. Therefore, those who receive so much grace, beyond and in spite of all they deserve, ought to acknowledge it with humble and thankful hearts. On the other hand, with the apostle they ought to adore (but certainly not inquisitively search into) the severity and justice of God's judgments on the others, who do not receive this grace.

Article 8: The Earnest Call of the Gospel

Nevertheless, all who are called through the gospel are called earnestly. For urgently and most genuinely God makes known in the Word what is pleasing to him: that those who are called should come to God. God also earnestly promises rest for their souls and eternal life to all who do come and believe.

Article 9: Human Responsibility for Rejecting the Gospel

The fact that many who are called through the ministry of the gospel do not come and are not brought to conversion must not be blamed on the gospel, nor on Christ, who is offered through the gospel, nor on God, who calls them through the gospel and even bestows various gifts on them, but on the people themselves who are called. Some in self-assurance do not even entertain the Word of life; others do entertain it but do not take it to heart, and for that reason, after the fleeting joy of a temporary faith, they relapse; others choke the seed of the Word with the thorns of life's cares and with the pleasures of the world and bring forth no fruits. This our Savior teaches in the parable of the sower (Matt. 13).

Article 10: Conversion as the Work of God

The fact that others who are called through the ministry of the gospel do come and are brought to conversion must not be credited to human effort, as though one distinguishes oneself by free choice from others who are furnished with equal or sufficient grace for faith and conversion (as the proud heresy of Pelagius maintains). No, it must be credited to God: just as from eternity God chose his own in Christ, so within time God effectively calls them, grants them faith and repentance, and, having rescued them from the dominion of darkness, brings them into the kingdom of his Son, in order that they may declare the wonderful deeds of the One who called them out of darkness into this marvelous light, and may boast not in themselves, but in the Lord, as apostolic words frequently testify in Scripture.

Article 11: The Holy Spirit's Work in Conversion

Moreover, when God carries out this good pleasure in the elect, or works true conversion in them, God not only sees to it that the gospel is proclaimed to them outwardly, and enlightens their minds powerfully by the Holy Spirit so that they may rightly understand and discern the things of the Spirit of God, but, by the effective operation of the same regenerating Spirit, God also penetrates into the inmost being, opens the closed heart, softens the hard heart, and circumcises the heart that is uncircumcised. God infuses new qualities into the will, making the dead will alive, the evil one good, the unwilling one willing, and the stubborn one compliant. God activates and strengthens the will so that, like a good tree, it may be enabled to produce the fruits of good deeds.

Article 12: Regeneration a Supernatural Work

And this is the regeneration, the new creation, the raising from the dead, and the making alive so clearly proclaimed in the Scriptures, which God works in us without our help. But this certainly does not happen only by outward teaching, by moral persuasion, or by such a way of working that, after God's work is done, it remains in human power whether or not to be reborn or converted. Rather, it is an entirely supernatural work, one that is at the same time most powerful and most pleasing, a marvelous, hidden, and inexpressible work, which is not less than or inferior in power to that of creation or of raising the dead, as Scripture (inspired by the author of this work) teaches. As a result, all those in whose hearts God works in this marvelous way are certainly, unfailingly, and effectively reborn and do actually believe. And then the will, now renewed, is not only activated and motivated by God, but in being activated by God is also itself active. For this reason, people themselves, by that grace which they have received, are also rightly said to believe and to repent.

Article 13: The Incomprehensible Way of Regeneration

In this life believers cannot fully understand the way this work occurs; meanwhile, they rest content with knowing and experiencing that, by this grace of God, they do believe with the heart and love their Savior.

Article 14: The Way God Gives Faith

In this way, therefore, faith is a gift of God, not in the sense that it is offered by God for people to choose, but that it is in actual fact bestowed on them, breathed and infused into them. Nor is it a gift in the sense that God bestows only the potential to believe, but then awaits assent—the act of believing—by human choice; rather, it is a gift in the sense that God who works both willing and acting and, indeed, works all things in all people and produces in them both the will to believe and the belief itself.

Article 15: Responses to God's Grace

God does not owe this grace to anyone. For what could God owe to those who have nothing to give that can be paid back? Indeed, what could God owe to those who have nothing of their own to give but sin and falsehood? Therefore those who receive this grace owe and give eternal thanks to God alone; those who do not receive it either do not care at all about these spiritual things and are satisfied with themselves in their condition, or else in self-assurance foolishly boast about having something which they lack. Furthermore, following the example of the apostles, we are to think and to speak in the most favorable way about those who outwardly profess their faith and better their lives, for the inner chambers of the heart are unknown to us. But for others who have not yet been called, we are to pray to the God who calls things that do not exist as though they did. In no way, however, are we to pride ourselves as better than they, as though we had distinguished ourselves from them.

Article 16: Regeneration's Effect

However, just as by the fall humans did not cease to be human, endowed with intellect and will, and just as sin, which has spread through the whole human race, did not abolish the nature of the human race but distorted and spiritually killed it, so also this divine grace of regeneration does not act in people as if they were blocks and stones; nor does it abolish the will and its properties or coerce a reluctant will by force, but spiritually revives, heals, reforms, and—in a manner at once pleasing and powerful—bends it back.

As a result, a ready and sincere obedience of the Spirit now begins to prevail where before the rebellion and resistance of the flesh were completely dominant. In this the true and spiritual restoration and freedom of our will consists. Thus, if the marvelous Maker of every good thing were not dealing with us, we would have no hope of getting up from our fall by our own free choice, by which we plunged ourselves into ruin when still standing upright.

Article 17: God's Use of Means in Regeneration

Just as the almighty work by which God brings forth and sustains our natural life does not rule out but requires the use of means, by which God, according to his infinite wisdom and goodness, has wished to exercise that divine power, so also the aforementioned supernatural work by which God regenerates us in no way rules out or cancels the use of the gospel, which God in great wisdom has appointed to be the seed of regeneration and the food of the soul. For this reason, the apostles and the teachers who followed them taught the people in a godly manner about this grace of God, to give God the glory and to humble all pride, and yet did not neglect meanwhile to keep the people, by means of the holy admonitions of the gospel, under the administration of the Word, the sacraments, and discipline. So even today it is out of the question that the teachers or those taught in the church should presume to test God by separating what God in his good pleasure has wished to be closely joined together. For grace is bestowed through admonitions, and the more readily we perform our duty, the more lustrous the benefit of God working in us usually is, and the better that work advances. To God alone, both for the means and for their saving fruit and effectiveness, all glory is owed forever. Amen.

Rejection of the Errors
Having set forth the orthodox teaching, the Synod rejects the errors of those

I
Who teach that, properly speaking, it cannot be said that original sin in itself is enough to condemn the whole human race or to warrant temporal and eternal punishments.

For they contradict the apostle when he says: "Sin entered the world through one man, and death through sin, and in this way death passed on to all people because all sinned" (Rom. 5:12); also: "The guilt followed one sin and brought condemnation" (Rom. 5:16); likewise: "The wages of sin is death" (Rom. 6:23).

II
Who teach that the spiritual gifts or the good dispositions and virtues such as goodness, holiness, and righteousness could not have resided in the human will at creation, and therefore could not have been separated from the will at the fall.

For this conflicts with the apostle's description of the image of God in Ephesians 4:24, where he portrays the image in terms of righteousness and holiness, which definitely reside in the will.

III
Who teach that in spiritual death the spiritual gifts have not been separated from human will, since the will in itself has never been corrupted but only hindered by the darkness of the mind and the unruliness of the emotions, and since the will is able to exercise its innate free capacity once these hindrances are removed, which is to say, it is able of itself to will or choose whatever good is set before it—or else not to will or choose it.

This is a novel idea and an error and has the effect of elevating the power of free choice, contrary to the words of Jeremiah the prophet: "The heart itself is deceitful above all things and wicked" (Jer. 17:9); and of the words of the apostle: "All of us also lived among them" (the children of disobedience) "at one time in the passions of our flesh, following the will of our flesh and thoughts" (Eph. 2:3).

IV

Who teach that unregenerate humanity is not strictly or totally dead in sin or deprived of all capacity for spiritual good but is able to hunger and thirst for righteousness or life and to offer the sacrifice of a broken and contrite spirit which is pleasing to God.

For these views are opposed to the plain testimonies of Scripture: "You were dead in your transgressions and sins" (Eph. 2:1, 5); "The imagination of the thoughts of the human heart is only evil all the time" (Gen. 6:5; 8:21). Besides, to hunger and thirst for deliverance from misery and for life, and to offer God the sacrifice of a broken spirit is characteristic only of the regenerate and of those called blessed (Ps. 51:17; Matt. 5:6).

V

Who teach that corrupt and natural humanity can make such good use of common grace (by which they mean the light of nature) or of the gifts remaining after the fall that they are able thereby gradually to obtain a greater grace—evangelical or saving grace—as well as salvation itself; and that in this way God, for his part, shows himself ready to reveal Christ to all people, since God provides to all, to a sufficient extent and in an effective manner, the means necessary for the revealing of Christ, for faith, and for repentance.

For Scripture, not to mention the experience of all ages, testifies that this is false: "He makes known his words to Jacob, his statutes and his laws to Israel; he has done this for no other nation, and they do not know his laws" (Ps. 147:19-20); "In the past God let all nations go their own way" (Acts 14:16); "They" (Paul and his companions) "were kept by the Holy Spirit from speaking God's word in Asia"; and "When they had come to Mysia, they tried to go to Bithynia, but the Spirit would not allow them to" (Acts 16:6-7).

VI

Who teach that in the true conversion of men and women new qualities, dispositions, or gifts cannot be infused or poured into their will by God, and indeed that the faith [or believing] by which we first come to conversion and from which we receive the name "believers" is not a quality or gift infused by God, but only a human act, and that it cannot be called a gift except in respect to the power of attaining faith.

For these views contradict the Holy Scriptures, which testify that God does infuse or pour into our hearts the new qualities of faith, obedience, and the experiencing of his love: "I will put my law in their minds, and write it on their hearts" (Jer. 31:33); "I will pour water on the thirsty land, and streams on the dry ground; I will pour out my Spirit on your offspring" (Isa. 44:3); "The love of God has been poured out in our hearts by the Holy Spirit, who has been given to us" (Rom. 5:5). They also conflict with the continuous practice of the church, which prays with the prophet: "Convert me, Lord, and I shall be converted" (Jer. 31:18).

VII
Who teach that the grace by which we are converted to God is nothing but a gentle persuasion, or (as others explain it) that the way of God's acting in conversion that is most noble and suited to human nature is that which happens by persuasion, and that nothing prevents this grace of moral persuasion even by itself from making the natural person spiritual; indeed, that God does not produce the assent of the will except in this manner of moral persuasion, and that the effectiveness of God's work by which it surpasses the work of Satan consists in the fact that God promises eternal benefits while Satan promises temporal ones.

For this teaching is entirely Pelagian and contrary to the whole of Scripture, which recognizes besides this persuasion also another, far more effective and divine way in which the Holy Spirit acts in human conversion. As Ezekiel 36:26 puts it: "I will give you a new heart and put a new spirit in you; and I will remove your heart of stone and give you a heart of flesh. . . ."

VIII
Who teach that God in regenerating people does not bring to bear that power of his omnipotence whereby God may powerfully and unfailingly bend the human will to faith and conversion, but that even when God has accomplished all the works of grace which he uses for their conversion, they nevertheless can, and in actual fact often do, so resist God and the Spirit in their intent and will to regenerate them, that they completely thwart their own rebirth; and, indeed, that it remains in their own power whether or not to be reborn.

For this does away with all effective functioning of God's grace in our conversion and subjects the activity of Almighty God to human will; it is contrary to the apostles, who teach that "we believe by virtue of the effective working of God's mighty strength" (Eph. 1:19), and that "God fulfills the undeserved good will of his kindness and the work of faith in us with power" (2 Thess. 1:11), and likewise that "his divine power has given us everything we need for life and godliness" (2 Pet. 1:3).

IX
Who teach that grace and free choice are concurrent partial causes which cooperate to initiate conversion, and that grace does not precede—in the order of causality—the effective influence of the will; that is to say, that God does not effectively help the human will to come to conversion before that will itself motivates and determines itself.

For the early church already condemned this doctrine long ago in the Pelagians, on the basis of the words of the apostle: "It does not depend on human willing or running but on God's mercy" (Rom. 9:16); also: "Who makes you different from anyone else?" and "What do you have that you did not receive?" (1 Cor. 4:7); likewise: "It is God who works in you to will and act according to his good pleasure" (Phil. 2:13).

The Fifth Main Point of Doctrine
The Perseverance of the Saints

Article 1: The Regenerate Not Entirely Free from Sin
Those people whom God according to his purpose calls into fellowship with his Son Jesus Christ our Lord and regenerates by the Holy Spirit, God also sets free from the dominion and slavery of sin, though not entirely from the flesh and from the body of sin as long as they are in this life.

Article 2: The Believer's Reaction to Sins of Weakness
Hence daily sins of weakness arise, and blemishes cling to even the best works of saints, giving them continual cause to humble themselves before God, to flee for refuge to Christ crucified, to put the flesh to death more and more by the Spirit of supplication and by holy exercises of godliness, and to strain toward the goal of perfection, until they are freed from this body of death and reign with the Lamb of God in heaven.

Article 3: God's Preservation of the Converted
Because of these remnants of sin dwelling in them and also because of the temptations of the world and Satan, those who have been converted could not remain standing in this grace if left to their own resources. But God is faithful, mercifully strengthening them in the grace once conferred on them and powerfully preserving them in it to the end.

Article 4: The Danger of True Believers' Falling into Serious Sins
The power of God strengthening and preserving true believers in grace is more than a match for the flesh. Yet those converted are not always so activated and motivated by God that in certain specific actions they cannot by their own fault depart from the leading of grace, be led astray by the desires of the flesh, and give in to them. For this reason they must constantly watch and pray that they may not be led into temptations. When they fail to do this, not only can they be carried away by the flesh, the world, and Satan

into sins, even serious and outrageous ones, but also by God's just permission they sometimes are so carried away—witness the sad cases, described in Scripture, of David, Peter, and other saints falling into sins.

Article 5: The Effects of Such Serious Sins
By such monstrous sins, however, they greatly offend God, deserve the sentence of death, grieve the Holy Spirit, suspend the exercise of faith, severely wound the conscience, and sometimes lose the awareness of grace for a time—until, after they have returned to the right way by genuine repentance, God's fatherly face again shines upon them.

Article 6: God's Saving Intervention
For God, who is rich in mercy, according to the unchangeable purpose of election does not take the Holy Spirit from his own completely, even when they fall grievously. Neither does God let them fall down so far that they forfeit the grace of adoption and the state of justification, or commit the sin which leads to death (the sin against the Holy Spirit), and plunge themselves, entirely forsaken by God, into eternal ruin.

Article 7: Renewal to Repentance
For, in the first place, God preserves in those saints when they fall the imperishable seed from which they have been born again, lest it perish or be dislodged. Secondly, by his Word and Spirit God certainly and effectively renews them to repentance so that they have a heartfelt and godly sorrow for the sins they have committed; seek and obtain, through faith and with a contrite heart, forgiveness in the blood of the Mediator; experience again the grace of a reconciled God; through faith adore God's mercies; and from then on more eagerly work out their own salvation with fear and trembling.

Article 8: The Certainty of This Preservation
So it is not by their own merits or strength but by God's undeserved mercy that they neither forfeit faith and grace totally nor remain in their downfalls to the end and are lost. With respect to themselves this not only easily could happen, but also undoubtedly would happen; but with respect to God it cannot possibly happen. God's plan cannot be changed; God's promise cannot fail; the calling according to God's purpose cannot be revoked; the merit of Christ as well as his interceding and preserving cannot be nullified; and the sealing of the Holy Spirit can neither be invalidated nor wiped out.

Article 9: The Assurance of This Preservation
Concerning this preservation of those chosen to salvation and concerning the perseverance of true believers in faith, believers themselves can and do become assured in accordance with the measure of their faith. By this faith they firmly believe that they are and always will remain true and living members of the church, and that they have the forgiveness of sins and eternal life.

Article 10: The Ground of This Assurance

Accordingly, this assurance does not derive from some private revelation beyond or outside the Word, but from faith in the promises of God which are very plentifully revealed in the Word for our comfort, from the testimony of "the Holy Spirit testifying with our spirit that we are God's children and heirs" (Rom. 8:16-17), and finally from a serious and holy pursuit of a clear conscience and of good works. If God's chosen ones in this world did not have this well-founded comfort that the victory will be theirs and this reliable guarantee of eternal glory, they would be of all people most miserable.

Article 11: Doubts Concerning This Assurance

Meanwhile, Scripture testifies that believers have to contend in this life with various doubts of the flesh, and that under severe temptation they do not always experience this full assurance of faith and certainty of perseverance. But God, the Father of all comfort, "does not let them be tempted beyond what they can bear, but with the temptation he also provides a way out" (1 Cor. 10:13), and by the Holy Spirit revives in them the assurance of their perseverance.

Article 12: This Assurance as an Incentive to Godliness

This assurance of perseverance, however, so far from making true believers proud and carnally self-assured, is rather the true root of humility, of child-like respect, of genuine godliness, of endurance in every conflict, of fervent prayers, of steadfastness in crossbearing and in confessing the truth, and of well-founded joy in God. Reflecting on this benefit provides an incentive to a serious and continual practice of thanksgiving and good works, as is evident from the testimonies of Scripture and the examples of the saints.

Article 13: Assurance No Inducement to Carelessness

Neither does the renewed confidence of perseverance produce immorality or lack of concern for godliness in those put back on their feet after a fall, but it produces a much greater concern to observe carefully the ways which the Lord prepared in advance. They observe these ways in order that by walking in them they may maintain the assurance of their perseverance, lest, by their abuse of God's fatherly goodness, the face of the gracious God (for the godly, looking upon that face is sweeter than life, but its withdrawal is more bitter than death) turn away from them again, with the result that they fall into greater anguish of spirit.

Article 14: God's Use of Means in Perseverance

And, just as it has pleased God to begin this work of grace in us by the proclamation of the gospel, so God preserves, continues, and completes this work by the hearing and reading of the gospel, by meditation on it, by its exhortations, threats, and promises, and also by the use of the sacraments.

Article 15: Contrasting Reactions to the Teaching of Perseverance

This teaching about the perseverance of true believers and saints, and about their assurance of it—a teaching which God has very richly revealed in the

Word for the glory of his name and for the comfort of the godly, and which God impresses on the hearts of believers—is something which the flesh does not understand, Satan hates, the world ridicules, the ignorant and the hypocrites abuse, and the spirits of error attack. The bride of Christ, on the other hand, has always loved this teaching very tenderly and defended it steadfastly as a priceless treasure; and God, against whom no plan can avail and no strength can prevail, will ensure that the church will continue to do this. To this God alone, Father, Son, and Holy Spirit, be honor and glory forever. Amen.

Rejection of the Errors Concerning the Teaching of the Perseverance of the Saints

Having set forth the orthodox teaching, the Synod rejects the errors of those

I

Who teach that the perseverance of true believers is not an effect of election or a gift of God produced by Christ's death, but a condition of the new covenant which people, before what they call their "peremptory" election and justification, must fulfill by their free will.

For Holy Scripture testifies that perseverance follows from election and is granted to the chosen by virtue of Christ's death, resurrection, and intercession: "The chosen obtained it; the others were hardened" (Rom. 11:7); likewise, "He who did not spare his own son, but gave him up for us all—how will he not, along with him, grant us all things? Who will bring any charge against those whom God has chosen? It is God who justifies. Who is he that condemns? It is Christ Jesus who died—more than that, who was raised—who also sits at the right hand of God, and is also interceding for us. Who shall separate us from the love of Christ?" (Rom. 8:32-35).

II

Who teach that God does provide believers with sufficient strength to persevere and is ready to preserve this strength in them if they perform their duty, but that even with all those things in place which are necessary to persevere in faith and which God is pleased to use to preserve faith, it still always depends on the choice of human will whether or not to persevere.

For this view is obviously Pelagian; and though it intends to make people free it makes them sacrilegious. It is against the enduring consensus of evangelical teaching which takes from humanity all cause for boasting and ascribes the praise for this benefit only to God's grace. It is also against the testimony of the apostle: "It is God who keeps us strong to the end, so that we will be blameless on the day of our Lord Jesus Christ" (1 Cor. 1:8).

III

Who teach that those who truly believe and have been born again not only can forfeit justifying faith as well as grace and salvation totally and to the end, but also in actual fact do often forfeit them and are lost forever.

For this opinion nullifies the very grace of justification and regeneration as well as the continual preservation by Christ, contrary to the plain words of the apostle Paul: "If Christ died for us while we were still sinners, we will therefore much more be saved from God's wrath through him, since we have now been justified by his blood" (Rom. 5:8-9); and contrary to the apostle John: "No one who is born of God is intent on sin, because God's seed remains in him, nor can he sin, because he has been born of God" (1 John 3:9); also contrary to the words of Jesus Christ: "I give eternal life to my sheep, and they shall never perish; no one can snatch them out of my hand. My Father, who has given them to me, is greater than all; no one can snatch them out of my Father's hand" (John 10:28-29).

IV
Who teach that those who truly believe and have been born again can commit the sin that leads to death (the sin against the Holy Spirit).

For the same apostle John, after making mention of those who commit the sin that leads to death and forbidding prayer for them (1 John 5:16-17), immediately adds: "We know that anyone born of God does not commit sin" (that is, that kind of sin), "but the one who was born of God keeps himself safe, and the evil one does not touch him" (v. 18).

V
Who teach that apart from a special revelation no one can have the assurance of future perseverance in this life.

For by this teaching the well-founded consolation of true believers in this life is taken away and the doubting of the Romanists is reintroduced into the church. Holy Scripture, however, in many places derives the assurance not from a special and extraordinary revelation but from the marks peculiar to God's children and from God's completely reliable promises. So especially the apostle Paul: "Nothing in all creation can separate us from the love of God that is in Christ Jesus our Lord" (Rom. 8:39); and John: "They who obey his commands remain in him and he in them. And this is how we know that he remains in us: by the Spirit he gave us" (1 John 3:24).

VI
Who teach that the teaching of the assurance of perseverance and of salvation is by its very nature and character an opiate of the flesh and is harmful to godliness, good morals, prayer, and other holy exercises, but that, on the contrary, to have doubt about this is praiseworthy.

For these people show that they do not know the effective operation of God's grace and the work of the indwelling Holy Spirit, and they contradict the apostle John, who asserts the opposite in plain words: "Dear friends, now we are children of God, but what we will be has not yet been made known. But we know that when he is made known, we shall be like him, for we shall see him as he is. Everyone who has this hope in him purifies himself, just as he is pure" (1 John 3:2-3). Moreover, they are refuted by the examples of the saints in both the Old and the New Testament, who though assured of their perseverance and salvation yet were constant in prayer and other exercises of godliness.

VII
Who teach that the faith of those who believe only temporarily does not differ from justifying and saving faith except in duration alone.

For Christ himself in Matthew 13:20ff. and Luke 8:13ff. clearly defines these further differences between temporary and true believers: he says that the former receive the seed on rocky ground, and the latter receive it in good ground, or a good heart; the former have no root, and the latter are firmly rooted; the former have no fruit, and the latter produce fruit in varying measure, with steadfastness, or perseverance.

VIII
Who teach that it is not absurd that people, after losing their former regeneration, should once again, indeed quite often, be reborn.

For by this teaching they deny the imperishable nature of God's seed by which we are born again, contrary to the testimony of the apostle Peter: "Born again, not of perishable seed, but of imperishable" (1 Pet. 1:23).

IX
Who teach that Christ nowhere prayed for an unfailing perseverance of believers in faith.

For they contradict Christ himself when he says: "I have prayed for you, Peter, that your faith may not fail" (Luke 22:32); and John the gospel writer when he testifies in John 17 that it was not only for the apostles, but also for all those who were to believe by their message that Christ prayed: "Holy Father, preserve them in your name" (v. 11); and "My prayer is not that you take them out of the world, but that you preserve them from the evil one" (v. 15).

Conclusion
Rejection of False Accusations

And so this is the clear, simple, and straightforward explanation of the orthodox teaching on the five articles in dispute in the Netherlands, as well as the rejection of the errors by which the Dutch churches have for some time been disturbed. This explanation and rejection the Synod declares to be derived from God's Word and in agreement with the confessions of the Reformed churches. Hence it clearly appears that those of whom one could hardly expect it have shown no truth, equity, and charity at all in wishing to make the public believe:

- that the teaching of the Reformed churches on predestination and on the points associated with it by its very nature and tendency draws the minds of people away from all godliness and religion, is an opiate of the flesh and the devil, and is a stronghold where Satan lies in wait for all people, wounds most of them, and fatally pierces many of them with the arrows of both despair and self-assurance;
- that this teaching makes God the author of sin, unjust, a tyrant, and a hypocrite; and is nothing but a refurbished Stoicism, Manicheism, Libertinism, and Turkism*;
- that this teaching makes people carnally self-assured, since it persuades them that nothing endangers the salvation of the elect, no matter how they live, so that they may commit the most outrageous crimes with self-assurance; and that on the other hand nothing is of use to the reprobate for salvation even if they have truly performed all the works of the saints;
- that this teaching means that God predestined and created, by the bare and unqualified choice of his will, without the least regard or consideration of any sin, the greatest part of the world to eternal condemnation; that in the same manner in which election is the source and cause of faith and good works, reprobation is the cause of unbelief and ungodliness; that many infant children of believers are snatched in their innocence from their mothers' breasts and cruelly cast into hell so that neither the blood of Christ nor their baptism nor the prayers of the church at their baptism can be of any use to them; and very many other slanderous accusations of this kind which the Reformed churches not only disavow but even denounce with their whole heart.

Therefore this Synod of Dort in the name of the Lord pleads with all who devoutly call on the name of our Savior Jesus Christ to form their judgment about the faith of the Reformed churches, not on the basis of false accusations gathered from here or there, or even on the basis of the personal statements of a number of ancient and modern authorities—statements which are also often either quoted out of context or misquoted and twisted to convey a different meaning—but on the basis of the churches' own official confessions and of the present explanation of the orthodox teaching which has been endorsed by the unanimous consent of the members of the whole Synod, one and all.

Moreover, the Synod earnestly warns the false accusers themselves to consider how heavy a judgment of God awaits those who give false testimony against so many churches and their confessions, trouble the consciences of the weak, and seek to prejudice the minds of many against the fellowship of true believers.

Finally, this Synod urges all fellow ministers in the gospel of Christ to deal with this teaching in a godly and reverent manner, in the academic institutions as well as in the churches; to do so, both in their speaking and writing, with a view to the glory of God's name, holiness of life, and the comfort of anxious souls; to think and also speak with Scripture according to the analogy of faith; and, finally, to refrain from all those ways of speaking which go beyond the bounds set for us by the genuine sense of the Holy Scriptures and which could give impertinent sophists a just occasion to scoff at the teaching of the Reformed churches or even to bring false accusations against it.

May God's Son Jesus Christ, who sits at the right hand of God and gives gifts to humanity, sanctify us in the truth, lead to the truth those who err, silence the mouths of those who lay false accusations against sound teaching, and equip faithful ministers of God's Word with a spirit of wisdom and discretion, that all they say may be to the glory of God and the building up of their hearers. Amen.

*Islam

The Belhar Confession

Prologue

The Belhar Confession has its roots in the struggle against apartheid in southern Africa. This "outcry of faith" and "call for faithfulness and repentance" was first drafted in 1982 by the Dutch Reformed Mission Church (DRMC). The DRMC took the lead in declaring that apartheid constituted a *status confessionis* in which the truth of the gospel was at stake.

The Dutch Reformed Mission Church formally adopted the Belhar Confession in 1986. It is now one of the "standards of unity" of the Uniting Reformed Church in Southern Africa (URCSA), formed in 1994 by the union of the Dutch Reformed Mission Church and the Dutch Reformed Church in Africa. The Belhar's theological confrontation of the sin of racism has made possible reconciliation among Reformed churches in southern Africa and has aided the process of reconciliation within the nation of South Africa.

The Belhar's relevance is not confined to southern Africa. It addresses three key issues of concern to all churches: unity of the church and unity among all people, reconciliation within church and society, and God's justice. As one member of the URCSA has said, "We carry this confession on behalf of all the Reformed churches. We do not think of it as ours alone."

The Belhar Confession was adopted by General Synod 2009 of the Reformed Church in America (RCA). It was then ratified by two-thirds of the RCA's classes and incorporated into the *Book of Church Order* as a doctrinal standard at the 2010 General Synod. The Belhar Confession was adopted by the Synod of the Christian Reformed Church in North America as an Ecumenical Faith Declaration in 2012.

Note: The following is a translation of the original Afrikaans text of the confession as it was adopted by the synod of the Dutch Reformed Mission Church in South Africa in 1986. In 1994 the Dutch Reformed Mission Church and the Dutch Reformed Church in Africa united to form the Uniting Reformed Church in Southern Africa (URCSA). This inclusive language text was prepared by the Office of Theology and Worship, Presbyterian Church (USA).

The Confession of Belhar (September 1986)

1. **We believe** in the triune God, Father, Son and Holy Spirit, who gathers, protects and cares for the church through Word and Spirit. This, God has done since the beginning of the world and will do to the end.

2. **We believe** in one holy, universal Christian church, the communion of saints called from the entire human family.

   We believe
   - that Christ's work of reconciliation is made manifest in the church as the community of believers who have been reconciled with God and with one another (Eph. 2:11-22);

- that unity is, therefore, both a gift and an obligation for the church of Jesus Christ; that through the working of God's Spirit it is a binding force, yet simultaneously a reality which must be earnestly pursued and sought: one which the people of God must continually be built up to attain (Eph. 4:1-16);
- that this unity must become visible so that the world may believe that separation, enmity and hatred between people and groups is sin which Christ has already conquered, and accordingly that anything which threatens this unity may have no place in the church and must be resisted (John 17:20-23);
- that this unity of the people of God must be manifested and be active in a variety of ways: in that we love one another; that we experience, practice and pursue community with one another; that we are obligated to give ourselves willingly and joyfully to be of benefit and blessing to one another; that we share one faith, have one calling, are of one soul and one mind; have one God and Father, are filled with one Spirit, are baptized with one baptism, eat of one bread and drink of one cup, confess one name, are obedient to one Lord, work for one cause, and share one hope; together come to know the height and the breadth and the depth of the love of Christ; together are built up to the stature of Christ, to the new humanity; together know and bear one another's burdens, thereby fulfilling the law of Christ that we need one another and upbuild one another, admonishing and comforting one another; that we suffer with one another for the sake of righteousness; pray together; together serve God in this world; and together fight against all which may threaten or hinder this unity (Phil. 2:1-5; 1 Cor. 12:4-31; John 13:1-17; 1 Cor. 1:10-13; Eph. 4:1-6; Eph. 3:14-20; 1 Cor. 10:16-17; 1 Cor. 11:17-34; Gal. 6:2; 2 Cor. 1:3-4);
- that this unity can be established only in freedom and not under constraint; that the variety of spiritual gifts, opportunities, backgrounds, convictions, as well as the various languages and cultures, are by virtue of the reconciliation in Christ, opportunities for mutual service and enrichment within the one visible people of God (Rom. 12:3-8; 1 Cor. 12:1-11; Eph. 4:7-13; Gal. 3:27-28; James 2:1-13);
- that true faith in Jesus Christ is the only condition for membership of this church.

Therefore, we reject any doctrine
- which absolutizes either natural diversity or the sinful separation of people in such a way that this absolutization hinders or breaks the visible and active unity of the church, or even leads to the establishment of a separate church formation;
- which professes that this spiritual unity is truly being maintained in the bond of peace while believers of the same confession are in effect alienated from one another for the sake of diversity and in despair of reconciliation;

- which denies that a refusal earnestly to pursue this visible unity as a priceless gift is sin;
- which explicitly or implicitly maintains that descent or any other human or social factor should be a consideration in determining membership of the church.

3. We believe
- that God has entrusted the church with the message of reconciliation in and through Jesus Christ, that the church is called to be the salt of the earth and the light of the world, that the church is called blessed because it is a peacemaker, that the church is witness both by word and by deed to the new heaven and the new earth in which righteousness dwells (2 Cor. 5:17-21; Matt. 5:13-16; Matt. 5:9; 2 Peter 3:13; Rev. 21-22).
- that God's lifegiving Word and Spirit has conquered the powers of sin and death, and therefore also of irreconciliation and hatred, bitterness and enmity, that God's lifegiving Word and Spirit will enable the church to live in a new obedience which can open new possibilities of life for society and the world (Eph. 4:17–6:23, Rom. 6; Col. 1:9-14; Col. 2:13-19; Col. 3:1–4:6);
- that the credibility of this message is seriously affected and its beneficial work obstructed when it is proclaimed in a land which professes to be Christian, but in which the enforced separation of people on a racial basis promotes and perpetuates alienation, hatred and enmity;
- that any teaching which attempts to legitimate such forced separation by appeal to the gospel, and is not prepared to venture on the road of obedience and reconciliation, but rather, out of prejudice, fear, selfishness and unbelief, denies in advance the reconciling power of the gospel, must be considered ideology and false doctrine.

Therefore, we reject any doctrine
- which, in such a situation, sanctions in the name of the gospel or of the will of God the forced separation of people on the grounds of race and color and thereby in advance obstructs and weakens the ministry and experience of reconciliation in Christ.

4. We believe
- that God has revealed himself as the one who wishes to bring about justice and true peace among people;
- that God, in a world full of injustice and enmity, is in a special way the God of the destitute, the poor and the wronged;
- that God calls the church to follow him in this, for God brings justice to the oppressed and gives bread to the hungry;
- that God frees the prisoner and restores sight to the blind;
- that God supports the downtrodden, protects the stranger, helps orphans and widows and blocks the path of the ungodly;
- that for God pure and undefiled religion is to visit the orphans and the widows in their suffering;

- that God wishes to teach the church to do what is good and to seek the right (Deut. 32:4; Luke 2:14; John 14:27; Eph. 2:14; Isa. 1:16-17; James 1:27; James 5:1-6; Luke 1:46-55; Luke 6:20-26; Luke 7:22; Luke 16:19-31; Ps. 146; Luke 4:16-19; Rom. 6:13-18; Amos 5);
- that the church must therefore stand by people in any form of suffering and need, which implies, among other things, that the church must witness against and strive against any form of injustice, so that justice may roll down like waters, and righteousness like an ever-flowing stream;
- that the church as the possession of God must stand where the Lord stands, namely against injustice and with the wronged; that in following Christ the church must witness against all the powerful and privileged who selfishly seek their own interests and thus control and harm others.

Therefore, we reject any ideology
- which would legitimate forms of injustice and any doctrine which is unwilling to resist such an ideology in the name of the gospel.

5. **We believe** that, in obedience to Jesus Christ, its only head, the church is called to confess and to do all these things, even though the authorities and human laws might forbid them and punishment and suffering be the consequence (Eph. 4:15-16; Acts 5:29-33; 1 Peter 2:18-25; 1 Peter 3:15-18).

Jesus is Lord.

To the one and only God, Father, Son and Holy Spirit, be the honor and the glory forever and ever.

Testimonies

Our Song of Hope

This contemporary statement of faith was approved by the General Synod of the Reformed Church in America in 1978. While not having confessional status, it is meant to give a hymn-like expression of our faith within the heritage of the three Reformed confessions, especially addressing the issues that confront the church today.

We sing to our Lord a new song;
We sing in our world a sure Hope:
   Our God loves this world,
     God called it into being,
     God renews it through Jesus Christ,
     God governs it by the Spirit.
God is the world's true Hope.

I.   Our Hope in the Coming of the Lord
1.   We are a people of hope
     waiting for the return of our Lord.
   God has come to us
     through the ancient people of Israel,
     as the true Son of God, Jesus of Nazareth,
     as the Holy Spirit at work in our world.
   Our Lord speaks to us now through the inspired Scriptures.
     Christ is with us day by day.

II. Our Song in a Hopeless World
2.   We know Christ to be our only hope.
   We have enmeshed our world in a realm of sin,
     rebelled against God,
     accepted inhuman oppression of humanity,
     and even crucified God's son.
   God's world has been trapped by our fall,
     governments entangled by human pride,
     and nature polluted by human greed.

III. Jesus Christ, Our Only Hope
3.   Our only hope is Jesus Christ.
   After we refused to live in the image of God,
   He was born of the virgin Mary,
     sharing our genes and our instincts,
     entering our culture, speaking our language,
     fulfilling the law of our God.
   Being united to Christ's humanity,
     we know ourselves when we rest in Him.

4.   Jesus Christ is the hope of God's world.
     In His death,
         the justice of God is established;
         forgiveness of sin is proclaimed.
     On the day of the resurrection,
         the tomb was empty; His disciples saw Him;
         death was defeated; new life had come.
         God's purpose for the world was sealed.

5.   Our ascended Lord gives hope for two ages.
     In the age to come, Christ is the judge,
         rejecting unrighteousness,
         isolating God's enemies to hell,
         blessing the new creation in Christ.
     In this age, the Holy Spirit is with us,
         calling nations to follow God's path,
         uniting people through Christ in love.

IV. Our Hope in God's Words
6.   The Holy Spirit speaks through the Scriptures.
     The Spirit has inspired Hebrew and Greek words,
         setting God's truth in human language,
         placing God's teaching in ancient cultures,
         proclaiming the Gospel in the history of the world.
     The Spirit speaks truly what the nations must know,
         translating God's word into modern languages,
         impressing it on human hearts and cultures.

7.   The Holy Spirit speaks through the Church,
         measuring its words by the canonical Scriptures.
     The Spirit has spoken in the ancient creeds,
         and in the confessions of the Reformation.
     The world is called to bear witness to Christ
         in faithfulness to the Scriptures,
         in harmony with the church of the ages,
         and in unity with all Christ's people.

8.   God's Spirit speaks in the world
         according to God's ultimate word in Christ.
     In every time and place,
         in ancient cities and distant lands,
         in technology and business,
         in art and education,
     God has not been left without a witness.
     The Word has entered where we have failed to go.

9.   In each year and in every place
         we expect the coming of Christ's Spirit.
     As we listen to the world's concerns,
         hear the cry of the oppressed,
         and learn of new discoveries,
     God will give us knowledge,
         teach us to respond with maturity,
         and give us courage to act with integrity.

V. Our Hope in Daily Life
10. As citizens we acknowledge the Spirit's work in human government
         for the welfare of the people,
         for justice among the poor,
         for mercy towards the prisoner,
         against inhuman oppression of humanity.
     We must obey God above all rulers,
         waiting upon the Spirit,
         filled with the patience of Christ.

11. We pray for the fruits of the Spirit of Christ
         who works for peace on earth,
         commands us to love our enemies,
         and calls for patience among the nations.
     We give thanks for God's work among governments,
         seeking to resolve disputes by means other than war,
         placing human kindness above national pride,
         replacing the curse of war with international self-control.

12. We hear the Spirit's call to love one another
         opposing discrimination of race or sex,
         inviting us to accept one another,
         and to share at every level
             in work and play,
             in church and state,
             in marriage and family,
         and so fulfill the love of Christ.

13. As male and female we look to the Spirit
     Who makes us the stewards of life
         to plan its beginning,
         to love in its living,
         and to care in its dying.
     God makes us the stewards of marriage
         with its lifelong commitment to love;
     yet God knows our frailty of heart.

14. The Spirit leads us into Truth--
    the Truth of Christ's salvation,
    into increasing knowledge of all existence.
        He rejoices in human awareness of God's creation
        and gives freedom to those on the frontiers of research.
    We are overwhelmed by the growth in our knowledge.
        While our truths come in broken fragments,
        we expect the Spirit to unite these in Christ.

VI. Our Hope in the Church

15. Christ elects the church
        to proclaim the Word and celebrate the sacraments,
        to worship God's name,
        and to live as true disciples.
    He creates a community
        to be a place of prayer,
        to provide rest for the weary,
        and to lead people to share in service.

16. The Holy Spirit sends the church
    to call sinners to repentance,
    to proclaim the good news
        that Jesus is personal Savior and Lord.
    The Spirit sends it out in ministry
        to preach good news to the poor,
        righteousness to the nations,
        and peace among all people.

17. The Holy Spirit builds one church,
        united in one Lord and one hope,
        with one ministry around one table.
    The Spirit calls all believers in Jesus
        to respond in worship together,
        to accept all the gifts from the Spirit,
        to learn from each other's traditions,
        to make unity visible on earth.

18. Christ places baptism in the world
    as a seal of God's covenant people,
        placing them in ministry,
        assuring them of the forgiveness of sins.
    God knows those who are baptized in Jesus' name,
        guiding the church gently to lead us,
        calling us back when we go astray,
        promising life amid trials and death.

19. Christ places the Lord's table in this world.
    Jesus takes up our bread and wine
        to represent His sacrifice,
    to bind His ministry to our daily work,
        to unite us in His righteousness.
    Here Christ is present in His world
        proclaiming salvation until He comes,
        a symbol of hope for a troubled age.

VII. Our Hope in the Age to Come

20. God saves the world through Jesus.
    Those who call on that name will have life.
    Christ's hand reaches out beyond those who say "Lord"
        to the infants who live in the atmosphere of faith,
        even to the farthest stars and planets all creation.
    The boundaries of God's love are not known,
        the Spirit works at the ends of the world
        before the church has there spoken a word.

21. God will renew the world through Jesus,
    who will put all unrighteousness out,
        purify the works of human hands,
        and perfect their fellowship in divine love.
    Christ will wipe away every tear;
        death shall be no more.
    There will be a new heaven and a new earth,
        and all creation will be filled with God's glory.

Our Prayer

Come, Lord Jesus:
    We are open to your Spirit.
    We await your full presence.
    Our world finds rest in you alone.

Our World Belongs to God
A Contemporary Testimony

This second edition of the Contemporary Testimony was approved by Synod 2008 of the Christian Reformed Church in North America. (The first edition was adopted by Synod 1986.) While not having confessional status, it is meant to give a hymn-like expression of our faith within the heritage of the Reformed confessions, especially addressing issues that confront the church today.

Preamble

1. As followers of Jesus Christ,
    living in this world—
    which some seek to control,
    and others view with despair—
    we declare with joy and trust:
    Our world belongs to God!

For God's ownership of all things, see Psalm 24:1 (quoted in 1 Cor. 10:26); Job 41:11; and Deuteronomy 10:14. That this is also "our world"—given to the human race to keep and care for—is one of the themes of the creation stories in Genesis 1 and 2.

2. From the beginning,
    through all the crises of our times,
    until the kingdom fully comes,
    God keeps covenant forever:
    Our world belongs to God!
    God is King: Let the earth be glad!
    Christ is victor: his rule has begun!
    The Spirit is at work: creation is renewed!
    Hallelujah! Praise the Lord!

For God's faithfulness, see, among many passages, Psalm 89; 117; 145; Romans 8:31-39; and Hebrews 10:23. For the victory of God in Christ and the rule of Christ, see 1 Corinthians 15:54-57; Philippians 2:9-11; and Revelation 1:13-18. For the Spirit's work renewing creation, see Genesis 1 and Romans 8.

3. Still, despair and rebellious pride fill the earth:
    some, crushed by failure
    or broken by pain,
    give up on life and hope and God;
    others, shaken,
    but still hoping for human triumph,
    work feverishly to realize their dreams.

As believers in God,
we also struggle with the spirits of this age,
resisting them in the power of the Spirit,
testing them by God's sure Word.

Psalm 2 expresses the rebellious spirit of the human race. See also Romans 1-3. Ephesians 6:10-17 describes the struggle of believers with the spirits of the age. On testing the spirits, see 1 John 4.

4. Our world, fallen into sin,
    has lost its first goodness,
    but God has not abandoned the work of his hands:
    our Maker preserves this world,
    sending seasons, sun, and rain,
    upholding all creatures,
    renewing the earth,
    promising a Savior,
    guiding all things to their purpose.

See Genesis 3; 9:8-16; Psalm 104, especially verse 30; Matthew 5:45; and Acts 14:17. For the promises of a Savior, see Genesis 3:15; Isaiah 7:14; 11:1-5; 42:1-7; 53; and Micah 5:2.

5. God holds this world
    with fierce love.
    Keeping his promise,
    he sends Jesus into the world,
    pours out the Holy Spirit,
    and announces the good news:
    sinners who repent and believe in Jesus
    live anew as members of the family of God—
    the firstfruits of a new creation.

For God's fierce love, see Hosea 11, especially verses 10-11. For statements of the gospel message, see John 3:1-21; Acts 2:36-39; Romans 10:7-11; and Ephesians 2:1-10. For "first-fruits," see Leviticus 23:9-14 and James 1:18.

6. We rejoice in the goodness of God,
    renounce the works of darkness,
    and dedicate ourselves to holy living.
    As covenant partners,
    set free for joyful obedience,
    we offer our hearts and lives
    to do God's work in the world.
    With tempered impatience,
    eager to see injustice ended,
    we expect the Day of the Lord.

We are confident
that the light
which shines in the present darkness
will fill the earth
when Christ appears.
Come, Lord Jesus.
Our world belongs to you.

Among the texts referenced in this paragraph, see Matthew 5:17-20, 48; John 1:1-5, 9-13; 3:19-21; Romans 12:1-2; Galatians 5:1, 13-25; 1 Thessalonians 4:16-5:11; 2 Peter 3; 1 John 2:7-11; and Revelation 22:20.

Creation

7. Our world belongs to God—
    not to us or earthly powers,
    not to demons, fate, or chance.
    The earth is the Lord's.

For references, see the first paragraph.

8. In the beginning, God—
    Father, Word, and Spirit—
    called this world into being
    out of nothing,
    and gave it shape and order.

See Genesis 1, where Creator, Word, and Spirit call creation into order. For the role of the Word in creation and Jesus as the Word, see John 1:1-14.

9. God formed sky, land, and sea;
    stars above, moon and sun,
    making a world of color, beauty, and variety—
    a fitting home for plants and animals, and us—
    a place to work and play,
    worship and wonder,
    love and laugh.
    God rested
    and gave us rest.
    In the beginning
    everything was very good.

On creation, besides Genesis 1 and 2, see Psalm 19; 33:6-9; and 104.

10. Made in God's image
   to live in loving communion with our Maker,
   we are appointed earthkeepers and caretakers
   to tend the earth, enjoy it,
   and love our neighbors.
   God uses our skills
   for the unfolding and well-being of his world
   so that creation and all who live in it may flourish.

For the image of God, see Genesis 1:26-27; 9:6; Ephesians 4:24; Colossians 3:10; and James 3:9.

11. Together,
   male and female,
   single and married,
   young and old—
   every hue and variety of humanity—
   we are called to represent God,
   for the Lord God made us all.
   Life is God's gift to us,
   and we are called to foster
   the well-being of all the living,
   protecting from harm
   the unborn and the weak,
   the poor and the vulnerable.

See Genesis 1:26-27; Galatians 3:26-28; and Acts 2:5-11. On how we treat the vulnerable among us as a measure of justice, see Isaiah 1:15-17 and James 1:27.

12. Even now,
   as history unfolds
   in ways we know only in part,
   we are assured
   that God is with us in our world,
   holding all things in tender embrace
   and bending them to his purpose.
   The confidence that the Lord is faithful
   gives meaning to our days
   and hope to our years.
   The future is secure,
   for our world belongs to God.

For the providential care of God, see Isaiah 45:6-7; Matthew 6:25-34; and Luke 12:4-7.

Fall

13. In the beginning of human history,
    our first parents walked with God.
    But rather than living by the Creator's word of life,
    they listened to the serpent's lie
    and fell into sin.
    In their rebellion
    they tried to be like God.
    As sinners, Adam and Eve feared
    the nearness of God
    and hid.

For the fall of humanity into sin, see Genesis 3. On the serpent, see, in addition to Genesis 3, Revelation 12:9 and 20:2.

14. Fallen in that first sin,
    we prove each day
    that apart from grace
    we are guilty sinners:
    we fail to thank God,
    we break God's laws,
    we ignore our tasks.
    Looking for life without God,
    we find death;
    grasping for freedom outside the law,
    we trap ourselves in Satan's snares;
    pursuing pleasure,
    we lose the gift of joy.

For the effects of the fall on humanity, see especially Romans 1:18-3:18.

15. When humans deface God's image,
    the whole world suffers:
    we abuse the creation or idolize it;
    we are estranged from our Creator,
    from our neighbor,
    from our true selves,
    and from all that God has made.

On the defacing of God's image, see Romans 1:21-23. For the restoration of the image in Christ, see Romans 8:29; 2 Corinthians 3:18; Ephesians 4:22-24; and Colossians 3:10.

16. All spheres of life—
    family and friendship,
    work and worship,
    school and state,
    play and art—
    bear the wounds of our rebellion.
    Sin is present everywhere—
    in pride of race,
    arrogance of nations,
    abuse of the weak and helpless,
    disregard for water, air, and soil,
    destruction of living creatures,
    slavery, murder, terror, and war,
    worship of false gods,
    the mistreatment of our bodies,
    and our frantic efforts to escape reality.
    We become victims of our own sin.

Among many passages, see Psalm 14; 53; Amos 1-2; Romans 1:28-32; and Galatians 5:19-21.

17. In all our striving
    to excuse or save ourselves,
    we stand condemned
    before the God of truth.
    But our world,
    broken and scarred,
    still belongs to God,
    who holds it together
    and gives us hope.

See Psalm 62; 89:28-37; Romans 5:3-11; 15:13; and Hebrews 11:1.

Redemption

18. While justly angry,
    God did not turn away
    from a world bent on destruction
    but turned to face it in love.
    With patience and tender care
    the Lord set out
    on the long road of redemption
    to reclaim the lost as his people
    and the world as his kingdom.

For God's response to sin, see Genesis 3:9-15; John 3:16; and Luke 1:68-75. For the aim to restore the kingdom, see Revelation 11:15.

19. Although Adam and Eve were expelled
    from the garden
    and their days burdened
    by the weight of sin,
    the Lord held on to them in love
    and promised to crush
    the evil forces
    they had unleashed.

For God's kindness to Adam and Eve, see Genesis 3:15-19.

20. When evil filled the earth,
    God judged it with a flood
    but rescued Noah and his family
    and animals of every kind.
    He covenanted with all creatures
    that seasons will continue
    and that such destruction
    will not come again
    until the last day
    when the Lord returns
    to make all things new.

For God's promise not to repeat the flood, see Genesis 9:8-17; 1 Peter 2; and 2 Peter 3. For the final renewal, see Revelation 21:1-5.

21. The Lord promised to be God
    to Abraham, Sarah, and their children,
    calling them to walk faithfully before him
    and blessing the nations through them.
    God chose Israel to show the glory of his name,
    the power of his love,
    and the wisdom of his ways.
    The Lord gave them the law
    through Moses
    and led them
    by rulers and teachers,
    shaping a people
    in whom God is revealed—
    a light to the nations.

For God's promise to Abraham and to his people Israel, see Genesis 12:1-3; Deuteronomy 7-8; and Romans 9. For Abraham's children as the light to the nations, see Micah 6:8 and Isaiah 60.

22. When Israel spurned God's love—
    lusting after other gods,
    trusting in power and wealth,
    and hurting the weak—
    God scattered them among the nations,
    yet kept a faithful remnant
    and promised them the Messiah:
    a prophet to speak good news,
    a king to crush evil and rule the earth with justice,
    a priest to be sacrificed for sinners.
    God promised to forgive their sins
    and give them a new heart and a new spirit,
    moving them to walk in his ways.

For the scattering, see 2 Chronicles 36 and Isaiah 10:1-11. For the promises, see Isaiah 53;
Jeremiah 31; and Ezekiel 36.

Christ

23. Remembering the promise
    to reconcile the world to himself,
    God joined our humanity in Jesus Christ—
    the eternal Word made flesh.
    He is the long-awaited Messiah,
    one with us
    and one with God,
    fully human and fully divine,
    conceived by the Holy Spirit
    and born of the virgin Mary.

For Jesus as the incarnate Son of God, see Luke 1:31-35; John 1:1-14; and Hebrews 1:2-3.

24. As the second Adam,
    Jesus chose the path we had rejected.
    In his baptism and temptations,
    teaching and miracles,
    battles with demons
    and friendships with sinners,
    Jesus lived a full and righteous human life before us.
    As God's true Son,
    he lovingly obeyed the Father
    and made present in deed and word
    the coming rule of God.

In Romans 5:12-21, Christ is designated the second Adam. Hebrews 2:10-18 and 4:14-5:2
teach about his life of righteous humanity. The announcement of the kingdom is found,
among other places, in Mark 1:1, 14-15.

25. Standing in our place,
    Jesus suffered during his years on earth,
    especially in the tortures of the cross.
    He carried God's judgment on our sin—
    his sacrifice removed our guilt.
    God raised him from the dead:
    he walked out of the grave,
    conqueror of sin and death—
    Lord of Life!
    We are set right with God,
    given new life,
    and called to walk with him
    in freedom from sin's dominion.

For Jesus' lifelong suffering, see Hebrews 5:7-10. All four of the gospel passion accounts portray the depths of his suffering on the cross. Jesus' resurrection victory is proclaimed often, especially in Matthew 28:1-10 and 1 Corinthians 15:20-28.

26. Being both divine and human,
    Jesus is the only mediator.
    He alone paid the debt of our sin;
    there is no other Savior.
    We are chosen in Christ
    to become like him in every way.
    God's electing love sustains our hope:
    God's grace is free
    to save sinners who offer nothing
    but their need for mercy.

Christ is shown to be our mediator in 1 Timothy 2:5 and Hebrews 9:11-15, and our only Savior in John 14:6 and Acts 4:12. For our election in Christ to be like Christ, see Romans 8:29; 2 Corinthians 3:18; and Ephesians 1:3-4.

27. Jesus ascended in triumph,
    raising our humanity to the heavenly throne.
    All authority, glory, and sovereign power
    are given to him.
    There he hears our prayers
    and pleads our cause before the Father.
    Blessed are all
    who take refuge in him.

For Christ's universal authority and intercession as ascended Lord, see Matthew 28:18; Psalm 2:12; 1 John 2:1-2; and Hebrews 7:25. For the ascension of our humanity with him, see Hebrews 4:14-16; Ephesians 1:20-22; 2:6; and Colossians 3:1-4.

The Spirit

28. At Pentecost, promises old and new are fulfilled.
    The ascended Jesus becomes the baptizer,
    drenching his followers with his Spirit,
    creating a new community
    where Father, Son, and Holy Spirit make their home.
    Revived and filled with the breath of God,
    women and men,
    young and old,
    dream dreams
    and see visions.

On the fulfillment of promises at Pentecost along with dreams and visions, see Acts 2:16-21.
On the ascended Jesus as baptizer and also the imagery of drenching in baptism of the Spirit,
see Luke 3:16; John 1:32-33; 20:22; and Acts 2:32-33. On the Spirit creating a new community, note Acts 2:41-47 following Pentecost. On the Father, Son, and Spirit making their home
with God's people, see John 14:15-24.

29. The Spirit renews our hearts
    and moves us to faith,
    leads us into truth,
    and helps us to pray,
    stands by us in our need,
    and makes our obedience fresh and vibrant.
    God the Spirit lavishes gifts on the church
    in astonishing variety—
    prophecy, encouragement, healing,
    teaching, service, tongues, discernment—
    equipping each member
    to build up the body of Christ
    and to serve our neighbors.

On the Spirit's work of renewing our hearts, see Titus 3:4-7; moving us to faith, Romans 5:1-5;
leading us into truth, John 16:13; helping us to pray, Romans 8:26-27; standing by us in our
need, Hebrews 2:18; and making our obedience fresh and vibrant, Romans 8:1-11. On the
Spirit's gifts, see 1 Corinthians 12 and Romans 12:3-8.

30. The Spirit gathers people
    from every tongue, tribe, and nation
    into the unity of the body of Christ.
    Anointed and sent by the Spirit,
    the church is thrust into the world,
    ambassadors of God's peace,
    announcing forgiveness and reconciliation,
    proclaiming the good news of grace.
    Going before them and with them,
    the Spirit convinces the world of sin
    and pleads the cause of Christ.
    Men and women, impelled by the Spirit,
    go next door and far away

into science and art,
media and marketplace—
every area of life,
pointing to the reign of God
with what they do and say.

On the gathering of all nations, see Revelation 7:9-17; on the Spirit and the church's mission, John 20:21-22; Luke 24:49; and Acts 1:8; on the church's mission as ambassadors, 2 Corinthians 5:18-21; on the work of the Spirit in the world, John 16:7-11; and on the breadth of the church's mission in the Spirit, Philippians 1:27-2:15.

Revelation

31. God gives this world
    many ways to know him.
    The creation shows his power and majesty.
    He speaks through prophets, poets, and apostles,
    and, most eloquently, through the Son.
    The Spirit, active from the beginning,
    moved human beings to write the Word of God
    and opens our hearts to God's voice.

For general revelation, see Romans 1 and Acts 14; for the inspiration of the Bible, see 1 Timothy 3:14-17 and 2 Peter 1:16-21; and for the full revelation in Christ, see Hebrews 1 and Colossians 1.

32. The Bible is the Word of God,
    the record and tool of his redeeming work.
    It is the Word of truth,
    breath of God,
    fully reliable in leading us
    to know God
    and to walk with Jesus Christ
    in new life.

For the nature of Scripture, see Luke 1:1-4; John 20:30-31; Acts 8:26-39; James 1:18; and references in paragraph 31.

33. The Bible tells the story
    of God's mighty acts
    in the unfolding
    of covenant history.
    As one revelation in two testaments
    the Bible reveals God's will
    and the sweep of God's redeeming work.
    Illumined and equipped by the Spirit,
    disciples of Jesus hear and do the Word,
    witnessing to the good news
    that our world belongs to God,
    who loves it deeply.

For God's mighty acts, see Acts 2 and 7. For our instruction, see Matthew 16:13-19; 1 Corinthians 10:1- 11; 2 Timothy 3:14-17; and James 1:19-27.

God's New People

34. In our world,
    where many journey alone,
    nameless in the bustling crowd,
    Satan and his evil forces
    seek whom they may scatter and isolate;
    but God, by his gracious choosing in Christ,
    gathers a new community—
    those who by God's gift
    put their trust in Christ.
    In the new community
    all are welcome:
    the homeless come home,
    the broken find healing,
    the sinner makes a new start,
    the despised are esteemed,
    the least are honored,
    and the last are first.
    Here the Spirit guides
    and grace abounds.

For the new community, see 1 Peter 2:4-7; for the attacks of Satan, 1 Peter 5:8-11; for the gracious welcome, Matthew 11:28-30 and 1 Peter 5:5-7.

35. The church is the fellowship of those
    who confess Jesus as Lord.
    She is the bride of Christ,
    his chosen partner,
    loved by Jesus and loving him:
    delighting in his presence,
    seeking him in prayer—
    silent before the mystery of his love.

For the confession, see Matthew 10:32-33. For the church as the bride of Christ, see Ephesians 2:6; 5:21-33; 1 John 3:11-17; 4:13-21; and Revelation 21:9.

36. Our new life in Christ
    is celebrated and nourished
    in the fellowship of congregations,
    where we praise God's name,
    hear the Word proclaimed,
    learn God's ways,
    confess our sins,
    offer our prayers and gifts,
    and celebrate the sacraments.

For the church's worship, see Matthew 6:5-15; 28:18-20; Acts 2:41-47; Romans 10; and 1 Corinthians 11:17-34.

37. God meets us in the sacraments,
    communicating grace to us
    by means of water, bread, and wine.
    In baptism,
    whether of the newly born
    or newly converted,
    God reminds and assures us
    of our union with Christ in covenant love,
    the washing away of our sin,
    and the gift of the Holy Spirit—
    expecting our love and trust in return.

Matthew 3:13-17, with Matthew 28:19, establishes baptism as a gospel sacrament. That baptism is for children as well as adults and is accompanied by the gift of the Spirit is indicated in Acts 2:28-29. Titus 3:5 calls baptism a washing away of sins. Romans 6:1-11 and Galatians 3:27 show how it forms us as members of Christ. 1 Corinthians 10:1-10 indicates that baptism in itself is not a guarantee of salvation.

38. In the Lord's Supper, Christ offers
    his own crucified body and shed blood
    to his people,
    assuring them a share
    in his death and resurrection.
    By the Holy Spirit, he feeds us
    with his resurrection life
    and binds us to each other
    as we share one loaf and cup.
    We receive this food gladly,
    believing, as we eat,
    that Jesus is our life-giving food and drink
    and that he will come again
    to call us to the wedding feast of the Lamb.

Matthew 26:17-29 and parallels establish the Lord's Supper as a gospel sacrament. On the meaning of the Lord's Supper, see 1 Corinthians 5:7-8; 8:1-13; 10:14-21; and 11:23-26. See also Jesus' strong words on his presence in the Lord's Supper in John 6:48-58.

39. The church is a gathering
    of forgiven sinners called to be holy.
    Saved by the patient grace of God,
    we deal patiently with others
    and together confess our need
    for grace and forgiveness.
    Restored in Christ's presence,
    shaped by his life,
    this new community lives out
    the ongoing story of God's reconciling love,
    announces the new creation,
    and works for a world of justice and peace.

On the church as a forgiven community called to be holy, see Ephesians 1:3-7; on dealing
with one another patiently, Galatians 6:1-5 and Colossians 3:12-14; on the need for confession and restoration, 1 John 1:8-2:6; and on living out God's reconciling love as part of a new
creation, 2 Corinthians 5:17-21 and 1 John 3:16-17.

40. We grieve that the church,
    which shares one Spirit, one faith, one hope,
    and spans all time, place, race, and language,
    has become a broken communion in a broken world.
    When we struggle
    for the truth of the gospel
    and for the righteousness God demands,
    we pray for wisdom and courage.
    When our pride or blindness
    hinders the unity of God's household,
    we seek forgiveness.
    We marvel that the Lord gathers the broken pieces
    to do his work
    and that he blesses us still
    with joy, new members,
    and surprising evidences of unity.
    We commit ourselves to seeking and expressing
    the oneness of all who follow Jesus,
    and we pray for brothers and sisters
    who suffer for the faith.

On the unity of the church, see John 17:20-23 and Ephesians 2:11-22; 4:1-16.

The Mission of God's People

41. Joining the mission of God,
    the church is sent
    with the gospel of the kingdom
    to call everyone to know and follow Christ
    and to proclaim to all
    the assurance that in the name of Jesus
    there is forgiveness of sin
    and new life for all who repent and believe.
    The Spirit calls all members
    to embrace God's mission
    in their neighborhoods
    and in the world:
    to feed the hungry,
    bring water to the thirsty,
    welcome the stranger,
    clothe the naked,
    care for the sick,
    and free the prisoner.
    We repent of leaving this work to a few,
    for this mission is central to our being.

On our part in God's mission, see Matthew 28:18-20; Luke 14:45-49; and John 17:18; on seeing our mission beyond our local community, Matthew 24:14 and Acts 13:1-3; on meeting the needs of people, Matthew 25:31-46 and Luke 4:18-19; and on the centrality of mission to our being, John 20:21.

42. In a world estranged from God,
    where happiness and peace are offered in many names
    and millions face confusing choices,
    we witness—
    with respect for followers of other ways—
    to the only one in whose name salvation is found:
    Jesus Christ.
    In Jesus, God reconciles the world to himself.
    God loves all creation;
    his compassion knows no bounds.

On the exclusive claims of Christ, see John 14:6 and Acts 4:12; on God's love and compassion for the world, see Matthew 9:36-38 and John 3:16.

43. Jesus Christ rules over all.
    To follow this Lord is
    to serve him wherever we are
    without fitting in,
    light in darkness,
    salt in a spoiling world.

On the rule of Christ over the whole world, see Philippians 2:9-11; Colossians 1:15-20; and Revelation 11:15; on being light, salt, and not fitting in, see Matthew 5:13-16 and Romans 12:1-2.

44. Life is a gift from God's hand,
    who created all things.
    Receiving this gift thankfully,
    with reverence for the Creator,
    we protest and resist
    all that harms, abuses, or diminishes the gift of life,
    whether by abortion, pollution, gluttony,
    addiction, or foolish risks.
    Because it is a sacred trust,
    we treat all life with awe and respect,
    especially when it is most vulnerable—
    whether growing in the womb,
    touched by disability or disease,
    or drawing a last breath.
    When forced to make decisions
    at life's raw edges,
    we seek wisdom in community,
    guided by God's Word and Spirit.

On respect for all life, see Deuteronomy 5:17; Psalm 104:14-30; and Psalm 139:14-16. On the fact that our very bodies are temples of the Holy Spirit, see 1 Corinthians 6:19-20.

45. Since God made us male and female in his image,
    we respect each other as equals,
    not flaunting or exploiting our sexuality.
    While our roles and capacities may differ,
    we are careful not to confine God's gifts and calling
    to the shape of our cultural patterns or expectations.
    Sexuality is disordered in our fallen world—
    brokenness, abuse, pornography, and loneliness are the result—
    but Christ's renewing work gives hope
    for order and healing
    and surrounds suffering persons
    with compassionate community.

Male and female, we are all made in God's image: Genesis 1:26-27 and Galatians 3:27. On sexual disorder as a result of sin, see Romans 1:24 and 1 Corinthians 6:15-20.

46. We are the family of God,
    serving Christ together in Christian community.
    Single for a time or a life,
    devoted to the work of God,
    we offer our love and service
    to the building of the kingdom.
    Married, in relationships of lifelong loyalty,
    we offer our lives to the same work:
    building the kingdom,
    teaching and modeling the ways of the Lord
    so our children may know

Jesus as Lord
and learn to use their gifts
in lives of joyful service.
In friendship and family life,
singleness and marriage,
as parents and children,
we reflect the covenant love of God.
We lament the prevalence of divorce
and of selfish individualism in our societies.
We belong to God.

See the apostle Paul's discussion of singleness and marriage in 1 Corinthians 7. On the importance of teaching and modeling the ways of the Lord, see Deuteronomy 6:4-9; Proverbs 22:6; and Ephesians 6:1-4. Jesus' teaching on divorce is found in Matthew 19:1-12 and Mark 10:1-12. That we together reflect the love of God is taught in John 13:34-35 and all of 1 John.

47. Serving the Lord
in whom all things hold together,
we support sound education in our communities,
and we foster schools and teaching
in which God's truth shines in all learning.
All students,
without regard to abilities, race, or wealth,
bear God's image
and deserve an education
that helps them use their gifts fully.

For the importance of education, see Deuteronomy 6:1-9 and Proverbs 4:1-9; for the need for God's light, Psalm 119:105; for the central place of Christ, Colossians 1:17; for equal acceptance, James 2:1-13.

48. Our work is a calling from God.
We work for more than wages
and manage for more than profit
so that mutual respect
and the just use of goods and skills
may shape the workplace.
While we earn or profit,
we love our neighbors by providing
useful products and services.
In our global economy
we advocate meaningful work
and fair wages for all.
Out of the Lord's generosity to us,
we give freely and gladly
of our money and time.

For the place of work, see Genesis 2:15; Exodus 20:9; Ephesians 6:5-9; and 2 Thessalonians 3:6-13. For justice in the workplace, Ezekiel 34 and James 5:1-5. For generosity, 2 Corinthians 9 and 1 Thessalonians 4:9-12.

49. Rest and leisure are gifts from God
    that relax us and set us free
    to discover and to explore.
    But we confess
    that often our addiction to busyness
    allows our tools and toys to invade our rest
    and that an internet world with its temptations
    distorts our leisure.
    Reminding each other that
    our Maker rested and gave us rest,
    we seek to rest more trustingly
    and to entertain ourselves more simply.

For rest, see Genesis 2:2-3 and Deuteronomy 5:12-15; for the discriminating use of leisure, Philippians 4:8-9 and Ephesians 4:17-32.

50. Grateful for advances
    in science and technology,
    we participate in their development,
    fostering care for creation
    and respect for the gift of life.
    We welcome discoveries that prevent or cure diseases
    and that help support healthy lives.
    We respect embryonic life,
    approaching each new discovery,
    whether of science or of medical technique,
    with careful thought,
    seeking the will of God.

In Genesis 1:28-31 and 9:1-7, God gives to humanity the right and responsibility to develop and care for creation; for a reflection on the limitations of human technology and need for divine wisdom, see Job 28; for the continuing goodness of creation and the need for a prayerful approach to what we use of it, see 1 Timothy 4:4-5.

51. We lament that our abuse of creation
    has brought lasting damage
    to the world we have been given:
    polluting streams and soil,
    poisoning the air,
    altering the climate,
    and damaging the earth.
    We commit ourselves
    to honor all God's creatures
    and to protect them from abuse and extinction,
    for our world belongs to God.

Genesis 1:28-29; 7:1-5; Psalm 8; and Romans 8:18-25 teach that we are entrusted with caring for the earth.

52. We obey God first;
     we respect the authorities that rule,
     for they are established by God:
     we pray for our rulers,
     and we work to influence governments—
     resisting them only when Christ and conscience demand.
     We are thankful for the freedoms
     enjoyed by citizens of many lands;
     we grieve with those who live under oppression,
     and we seek for them the liberty to live without fear.

Romans 13:1-7 teaches respect for governing authorities (see also 1 Pet. 2:13-17); Revelation 13 illustrates government gone wrong; Colossians 1:16 teaches that authority and power come from Christ; Ephesians 6:12 warns us that authority and power can become infected by evil.

53. We call on all governments to do public justice
     and to protect the rights and freedoms
     of individuals, groups, and institutions
     so that each may do their tasks.
     We urge governments and pledge ourselves
     to safeguard children and the elderly
     from abuse and exploitation,
     to bring justice to the poor and oppressed,
     and to promote the freedom
     to speak, work, worship, and associate.

That governments are called to justice generally and that how a government treats the poor and the weak is a key indicator of a society's commitment to justice is taught in all the prophets and in psalms like Psalm 72.

54. Followers of the Prince of Peace
     are called to be peacemakers,
     promoting harmony and order
     and restoring what is broken.
     We call on our governments to work for peace
     and to restore just relationships.
     We deplore the spread of weapons
     in our world and on our streets
     with the risks they bring
     and the horrors they threaten.
     We call on all nations to reduce their arsenals
     to what is needed
     in the defense of justice and freedom.
     We pledge to walk in ways of peace,
     confessing that our world belongs to God;
     he is our sure defense.

Isaiah 2:1-4 expresses God's will for peace, and Jesus said, "Blessed are the peacemakers . . ." (Matt. 5:9).

New Creation

55. Our hope for a new creation is not tied
      to what humans can do,
      for we believe that one day
      every challenge to God's rule
      will be crushed.
      His kingdom will fully come,
      and the Lord will rule.
      Come, Lord Jesus, come.

On this hope, see 1 Peter 1:3-12; 2 Peter 3:3-13; 1 Thessalonians 4:13-5:11; and Revelation 11:15.

56. We long for that day
      when our bodies are raised,
      the Lord wipes away our tears,
      and we dwell forever in the presence of God.
      We will take our place in the new creation,
      where there will be no more death
      or mourning or crying or pain,
      and the Lord will be our light.
      Come, Lord Jesus, come.

For the coming of the kingdom of God, see Matthew 24; Acts 1:10-11; 1 Thessalonians 4:13-5:11; and Revelation 19:11-16. 1 Corinthians 15 speaks of the resurrection of the body; Revelation 21:4 of the wiping away of tears; and Revelation 21:22-27 of the light of heaven.

57. On that day
      we will see our Savior face to face,
      sacrificed Lamb and triumphant King,
      just and gracious.
      He will set all things right,
      judge evil, and condemn the wicked.
      We face that day without fear,
      for the Judge is our Savior,
      whose shed blood declares us righteous.
      We live confidently,
      anticipating his coming,
      offering him our daily lives—
      our acts of kindness,
      our loyalty, and our love—
      knowing that he will weave
      even our sins and sorrows
      into his sovereign purpose.
      Come, Lord Jesus, come.

Revelation 5 describes the Lion and the Lamb. For the just judgments of the Lord, see Revelation 19:1-10. A picture of the multitude of those declared righteous in Christ is found in Revelation 7:9-17. The concept of God weaving all things together is found, among other places, in Romans 8:28-39.

58. With the whole creation
    we join the song:
    "Worthy is the Lamb, who was slain,
    to receive power and wealth
    and wisdom and strength
    and honor and glory and praise!"
    He has made us a kingdom of priests
    to serve our God,
    and we will reign on earth.
    God will be all in all,
    righteousness and peace will flourish,
    everything will be made new,
    and every eye will see at last
    that our world belongs to God.
    Hallelujah! Come, Lord Jesus!

For the imagery of this paragraph, see Exodus 19:5-6; Isaiah 40; 1 Peter 2:9-10; and Revelation 4-5.